Chichester in the **1950s**

by
Edward Brown

FOREWORDS

BY HIS GRACE, THE DUKE OF RICHMOND AND GORDON, GOODWOOD

"This is the Chichester my father, the 9th Duke, so fondly remembered in the City, knew and loved. I was then in my Twenties and now I cannot help being nostalgic as I look back nearly half a century. The book shows it was, indeed, an important decade and Chichester should be grateful to the author for going to the trouble of recording the events in such detail with good pictures and chatty text.

"Here you can savour the long lost atmosphere of those post war years, when there was such great community spirit and love of the Sovereign, country, county and home town was paramount.

"So it is a very timely publication and, as a social record, it will surely be of increasing value to succeeding generations. Thank you, Mr. Brown, for a history with a difference."

BY THE RT. WORSHIPFUL THE MAYOR OF CHICHESTER,
Councillor Mrs. Clare Apel.

"Chichester, as I said in my inaugural speech, is a gem of a City, with its Georgian architecture, its Cathedral, the Cross and the Pallants. It is one of the delights of Sussex. But a city is more, much more than its architecture; it is a community, it is its memories.

"For me, the Fifties started with Sir Stafford Cripps (a name to frighten children at bed-time) and ended with Harold Macmillan and 'You've never had it so good'. In between were the Coronation, Suez, stilettos and rock and roll.

"Mr. Brown has put together a wonderful collection of essays together with beautiful photographs and illustrations which bring to life Chichester in that period of transition from austerity to affluence, from conscription to consumerism.

"Much has been published on Chichester in the war and indeed the pre-war City. This new work will not only bring pleasure and fond recollections, but will, I feel, be of enduring value to this and future generations. It has obviously been a real labour of love."

BY THE LORD BISHOP OF CHICHESTER,
The Rt. Rev. Eric Kemp, D.D.

"There is always much of interest, and some things of importance, which escape the history books because they exist only in the memory of some who lived at the time.

"It is, therefore, particularly valuable that a person such as Mr. Brown should commit to paper his reminiscences of an important period in our history and some very interesting characters who lived in it.

"It will be of real interest to many people at the present time and may well be of substantial use to future social historians of the mid-twentieth century.

"I commend the book warmly."

an introduction to

Chichester in the **1950s**

NOSTALGIC MEMORIES OF AN EVENTFUL DECADE

Many changes made the Fifties in Chichester a memorable decade. Pleasure was mixed with sadness as the City coped with all the post-war developments, but carrying it through was strong community spirit.

Recovery from the war was proving slow and tortuous and the A-bomb, Korean War, Stalinism and the Suez crisis cast shadows over everyone's lives.

Private businesses started to disappear in the Fifties. Streets filled with traffic, resulting in the first car parks. New schools and factories were built. Political intrigue entered the Council Chamber.

Big changes in the Services were the departure of the fighter squadrons from Tangmere and the absorption of the proud Royal Sussex Regiment into the New Army.

Rationing and controls lingered and National Service continued. There were shortages, queues and waiting lists for hospital operations, phones and cars. It was not until 1957 that Harold Macmillan became Prime Minister and started to produce the 'Never had it so good' years.

Two welcome developments were the building of the Bus Station and the long overdue re-building of the Railway Station. Gala Day was born. Chichester twinned with Chartres. The Festival Theatre was planned. Thanks to successful 1s. a week football lotteries, a new Roman Catholic Church was built and a swimming pool seemed at last a possibility.

Although the dream of an arts centre did not materialise, culture was to the fore with the successful 1951 Festival of Britain, the revival of the Music Festival and the open air performance of Merrie England. Petula Clark rose to fame.

But social organizations suffered from the sale of Kimbells and the closure of the Assembly Rooms for refurbishment. TV spelled doom for the cinemas.

Prices did not change much and food, beer, cigarettes and road tax (£12.2s.0d.) look cheap today. A three-bedroom house could be built for £2,200.

Celebrations of the Queen's Coronation in 1953 were splendid and colourful. Another highlight of the decade was a visit by the Queen and Duke of Edinburgh in 1956 when love of the Royal Family was universal.

It now seems remarkable that for much of the period there were half-a-dozen garages all practically within sight of the Cross. The City Council, which then had considerable powers, made big improvements to the Cattle Market and it became an important source of commerce every Wednesday.

The renowned Bishop Bell, who had taken the name of Chichester far and wide, retired and died in 1958. The 1950 closure of the Oliver Whitby School (now A&N) was particularly sad, remembering it dated back to 1712.

OUR PET, A STAR

Chichester singer and actress Petula Clark, famed for her 'Downtown' hit, rocketed to international stardom. By 1952, when 19, she had given 1,000 performances before one million people.

Radio listeners wanted more of the 'Girl with a voice like chapel bells.' Remarkably, over 68 million of her albums and singles have since been sold, proving she is among the most popular female performers.

Our Pet was not actually born in the City, but most of the family lived within the city walls. Her parents, Leslie and Doris Clark, were in Priory Road and her grandparents were born and bred in Chichester.

She wrote to the author: "I spent a lot of my childhood in Chichester when my grandparents were alive and I have a very soft spot for the City. I sent my son, Patrick, to the Prebendal School, where he was very happy, and now he, too, enjoys going back. I still visit Chichester often and have relatives living in the area."

STARRY EYED MiCHAEL

Well known film, stage and TV star Michael Elphick, pictured as a happy seven-year-old Chichester boy in 1953. Born in Litten House, St. Pancras, he went to St. James Infants School, progressing to the Central School and Lancastrian School, where he was head boy. His widowed mother, Mrs. Joan Elphick, recalled, "He always wanted to be an actor, but his headmaster was not encouraging, telling him he had stars in his eyes. They were more helpful at the Festival Theatre, where he worked as an electrician, and, at 18, he won a scholarship to drama school."

Two of the many school plays, in which he showed early talent, were 'Mid-Summer Night's Dream' and 'Merchant of Venice'.

FESTiVAL THEATRE SHOCK

A man with money walked out of an early planning meeting for the Festival Theatre in 1959. There was a poignant hush, but Leslie Evershed-Martin, who had got the idea from a TV programme, was not deterred and the Impossible Theatre became a reality three exciting years later. Wealthy London businessman George Booth of Funtington, showed early interest by offering £500 for secretarial expenses. But during an exploratory meeting in the Dolphin and Anchor Hotel in December 1959 he left saying he would not give any more. It was not viable.

"Mr. Evershed-Martin, regretted the set-back, but said it was not the end," recalled amateur actor and producer Geoffrey Marwood, who was one of those present. "So began the money-raising struggle. At the same time there was an appeal for a swimming pool and, unfortunately, a theatre caucus and a swimming pool caucus divided the city."

The first idea was to build a permanent stage and seat the audience in a marquee. That was costed at £17,000 and efforts were made to get 17 people to put up £1,000 each. Later the plan changed in favour of a permanent building and the eventual bill was £130,000. That was all met by private donations.

CiTY LiKED THE OPERAS

Enthusiastic Operatic Society members countered the effects of TV by entertaining productions of the timeless satire and lilting melodies of Gilbert and Sullivan operas. Inspired by Margaret Pink's dedication and skill, they cheerfully overcame the Assembly Rooms' limitations.

'MERRIE ENGLAND' CHORUS OF TOWNSFOLK

West Sussex artistic history was made in 1952 by the wonderful open-air performance of Merrie England in the perfect setting of Priory Park. The cast of over 100, drawn from local societies, was headed by the famous Anne Ziegler and Webster Booth with professionals Leslie Rands and Marjorie Eyre.

The like of the singing and acting, the costumes, scenery and lighting, has not been seen in the area since. Pessimists who thought it too ambitious were proved wrong because approaching 10,000 attended on the six evenings with the result that £566 was made for Chichester Eventide Housing Association's Donnington Home. The Society owed much to the Pink family, of mineral water fame, particularly Margaret Pink, the company's managing director. She had a very professional approach, filling the triple role of producer, musical director and conductor with accomplishment. Her successor, Jeanne Bevis, recalled, "She was a perfectionist, somebody very difficult to follow. But, although she was a strong character, not delegating anything to anybody, we all admired her." Compared with £5 in the Nineties, seat prices for the Fifties' shows seem cheap at 5s.6d., 3s.6d. and 2s.6d. They were put up to 6s.6d., 4s.6d. and 3s. in 1957.

MUSiC FESTiVAL SUCCESSES

Three successful competitors in a Fifties Chichester Music Festival :

VANESSA SMITH

JONATHAN SCOTT

KEITH COMINS

When the Festival was thankfully revived in 1955, after a 10 year gap, there were 268 competitors for the two dozen trophies and silver medals. The two day feast of music provided by piano, dancing, vocal, choral, string, elocution, recorder and orchestral classes attracted 2,000 visitors.

Acting as sponsors, Robert Davies Oratorio Choir raised the £180 expenses by events, which included a jumble sale and tea parties.

SWiMMiNG POOL iN A CiNEMA

A large static water tank, constructed in Oaklands Park for war-time fire fighting purposes, was often regarded as the answer to Chichester's swimming pool problem, especially as it was of Olympic size. Athletes wanted it to be the first stage of a sports centre, but this idea was too grandiose for councillors in financially difficult times.

To the surprise of many, the project which went ahead after 30 years of talk was putting the pool inside the Eastgate Square cinema. That was not cheap, for it cost £35,000 to buy the old Gaumont and thousands more to convert it. The public helped by chipping in £30,000 raised in three years by a 1s. a week football lottery.

Trustee Savings Bank manager, David Thomas, an ex-Bevin boy, was one of those behind this and his widow, Eileen, recalled, "It forced the Council to act. Many voluntary collectors had worked hard to make a contribution that could not be ignored." Praise for the cinema conversion in 1968 was not universal. David and Eileen Daughtry, who became prominent in the Cormorant Swimming Club, recalled: "The Council dragged its feet and when they eventually decided to go ahead, they made the big mistake of putting it in the cinema. It should have been in Oaklands Park."

COUNCiL'S £17,000 DEAL FOR BARRETTS

On a corner right by the City Cross, W.H. Barrett's century old bookshop, here seen decorated for the 1953 Coronation, was bought by the City Council for £17,000. Councillors wanted to control the development of the key site, by making sure a visual stop was created.

The Council acted quickly, buying the shop, which belonged to an ailing Lavant woman, the day after making the decision. Later a strip of land at the side was bought from the Cathedral authorities for £4,000.

According to Maurice Evans, one of the councillors, who took the decision, it was a wise move because the city got a well designed building (Russell and Bromley), safeguarding an important view of the Cathedral, and making a good investment. In fact, the Council disposed of the sorry-looking building and the land to Russell and Bromley, who were nextdoor, for £24,000.

RATiONiNG WENT ON

In the pre-supermarket days of the Fifties there were about a dozen grocers in the main streets, offering customers personal, friendly service. Staff in starched white aprons worked long hours for what today seems little pay. They weighed up goods individually and delivered weekly orders by van or cycle.

Rationing and shortages were all part of the scene. While clothes rationing ended in February 1949, meat, dairy products, and sugar were still restricted and it was not until July 1954 that all rationing ceased.

Cecil Green remembered starting in the trade as a 2s.6d. a week apprentice, rising to 3s. in the second year and 7s.6d. in the third year.

Grocers in the main streets included Home and Colonial, International Stores, David Greig, Harris and Hall, Worlds Stores, Maypole, Sharp Garland, Kimbells, Shippams, the Co-operative and Osbornes. They all did good trade, the International. employing about 15 with two delivery vans.

Back bacon was 11d. per lb., butter 10d., margarine 4d. and sugar 2d. At Lewis, tobacconist and confectioner, East Street, where Mr. Green's wife, Elsie, was manageress, a packet of Players cigarettes cost 11d. Chocolate bars were 1d., a box of chocolates 1s.11d. and ice-cream cones 2d.

NEW QUEEN PROCLAiMED

Demonstrating the universal love felt for the Royal Family, thousands gathered round the City Cross in February 1952 for the Queen's proclamation ceremony. Like the whole nation, the City had been in mourning for the death of King George V1, but, gradually, feelings of hope and expectancy emerged at the prospect of a new Elizabethan age.

A fanfare by the City Band heralded the reading by Mayor Russell Purchase of the archaic phrases of the proclamation. With bayonets fixed, Royal Sussex Regiment troops and Tangmere RAF men formed a guard of honour.

Signs of mourning were everywhere. Shops and cinemas closed. Social gatherings and meetings were cancelled. Bells tolled for special services, which hundreds attended. On the day of the King's funeral there was an impressive hour long service with a moving address by Bishop Bell in the Cathedral.

CORONATION DAY, JUNE 2 1953, was one of great joy with a carnival procession, fireworks display, street parties, and children's sports among the entertaining events.

Over £2,000, equal to 3d. on the rates, was spent on the celebrations, an amount which was criticised, particularly by Keates Estate Ratepayers' Association. Sports events organised by Chichester Athletic Club drew 800 children to Priory Park. Each of the City's 3,500 children received a 2s. coronation mug.

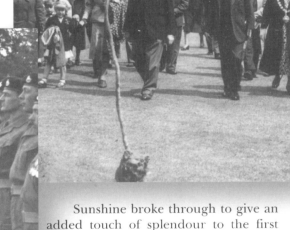

CORONATION TREE PLANTING

Thousands lined the streets in the evening to cheer a half-mile long carnival procession. Organised by St. Pancras, Whyke and Portfield Community Associations, this was one of the most splendid seen for years.

The memorable day ended with a £170 fireworks display on the Recreation Ground.

ROYAL INSPECTION PRIORY PARK 1956

Sunshine broke through to give an added touch of splendour to the first official Royal Visit for half a century. Enthusiastic crowds were warm and spontaneous in their welcome as the Queen and Duke of Edinburgh spent two hours in the City on July 30 1956. The pleasure of the day had been threatened by an unprecedented storm, which damaged the £1,500 worth of street decorations, but only a slight shower fell as the Queen replied to a loyal address in Priory Park.

An immaculate 96-strong guard of honour gave the Royal Salute and the band of the Royal Sussex Regiment's 1st. Battalion played the National Anthem.

Looking relaxed, the youthful Queen packed a lot into the programme, visiting the Guildhall Museum, 13th century St. Mary's Hospital, the Assembly Rooms, the Cathedral and the Bishop's Palace, where two commemorative trees were planted. Celebrations in Priory Park during the evening included open-air dancing.

CATHEDRAL TREES AXED

Axes were taken to the 80-year-old Cathedral lime trees in December 1951 and here is the first to be sent sprawling across the green. In the conservation Nineties it seems sacrilegious, but the Cathedral and City authorities wanted to fell trees in order to provide an open space, enhancing views of the Cathedral.

Controversy raged and a protest petition, organised by Parklands music teacher Miss Yvonne Godfrey was signed by 11,000 people countrywide. Happily, a compromise was reached and nine of the 16 trees were spared after consultations with the architect J.L. Denman.

CURTAINS FOR THE CINEMAS

Problems mounted for the City's three cinemas, Gaumont, Odeon and Granada, during the decade and, despite wide screen and technicolor advances, it was curtains for the Gaumont and Odeon in 1960. Sadly, audiences were depleted by TV. Overheads increased and redecorations costing thousands were ordered by licensing magistrates.

Chichester got the latest films and half a million people went to the pictures every year. The fire authorities were assured a cinema could be emptied in three minutes.

The purpose-built Gaumont seated 1,200, the Odeon 1,066 and the Granada 800. For epics there could be a hundred or so queuing in the street, even in rain. Today's prices make the seats seem cheap: 1s.3d. for front stalls, 1s.9d. for back stalls, 2s.4d. for the back circle and 3s. for the front circle.

Retired Odeon manager Fred Gompertz recalled, "When the shows finished after 10pm the City became happily full as friends met and exchanged views on the performances. Traffic flowed through the streets and there were buses home. Villagers travelling by cycle trustingly left their machines against the cinema walls."

Occasionally, stars made personal stage appearances. Among them were Petula Clark, Margaret Lockwood, Leo Genn, Michael Trubshawe and Diana Sheridan. Stirling Moss came in with a friend and sat in the front circle, relaxing with a friend before the next day's racing at Goodwood.

the odeon

ODEON STAGE PRESENTATION

Bishop Bell was so impressed by the Martin Luther film he suggested clergy should see it. Many dog collars were seen at the box office as vicars and curates came in large numbers for a matinee.

'A Queen is crowned', featuring the Coronation, was memorable. The Queen Mother's cousin, who had been involved in the ceremony, wanted to see street scenes he had missed.

Seat slashers were a problem for Gaumont manager Ron Savage. Wanton vandalism caused £100 worth of damage in five years. Eighty seats had to be replaced and another 80 repaired.

Rock 'n' Roll became a new musical craze and the Mid-Fifties film, 'Rock around the Clock', got jiving teenagers digging madly. They cheered, clapped and whistled at the Gaumont to the gems of Bill Haley and his Comets. Couples had to be restrained from getting into the aisles and after the show some were boisterously jiving in the streets.

It was not a thrilling Western, war epic or dazzling musical which broke all records. Two Billy Graham crusade films attracted over 13,000 people to the Gaumont during six days in February 1955. A Chichester crusade committee, chaired by St. Pancras Rector, the Rev. J. Marshall, was set up and hired the cinema at a cost of £550. After each showing people were invited to make a decision to follow Christ and 600 did so. "A lamp has been lit in Chichester which must not be allowed to go out," said Bishop Bell at a winding-up rally.

Audience decline made rationalisation look obvious and by the decade's end the heyday was over. In time, the Odeon became a supermarket, the Gaumont a swimming pool and the Granada, where Robbie Robinson was manager, a restaurant.

GLOBE TROTTiNG BiSHOP

Modest and reserved though he looked, Bishop George Bell was a powerful figure in the Church world-wide, showing great sincerity and energy, never afraid to speak his mind. During 29 years as Bishop of Chichester he took the City's name all over the world as he worked for the great causes of unity, peace and justice.

He held a unique place in the Church, a 20th century disciple fighting for peace in a world threatened by atomic destruction. Yet he cared greatly for his clergy and their flocks in Sussex. Chichester was privileged to have him and his wife, Henrietta, for so long. Some thought he might have been chosen as Archbishop of Canterbury in succession to Archbishop Temple in 1944, but the Establishment was unlikely to have a Primate so outspoken, unlikely, perhaps, to follow the official line.

Resentment built up over his speech against the blanket bombing of German towns, but, in fact, he drew a distinction between Germans and Nazis.

DEAN DUNCAN-JONES   BISHOP BELL

In 1954, he was appointed Honorary President of the World Council of Churches and Chichester made him an Honorary Freeman, Mayor Alice Eastland presenting him with a silver inkstand during a public ceremony.

There were many sides to the Bishop's character. A firm believer in trade unions, he addressed the annual dinner of NUPE (National Union of Public Employees) at Chichester in March 1956 and was made an Honorary Member. He intervened in a dispute with a parish council over a grave digger's dismissal.

With his extraordinary capacity for working long hours his secretary, Mrs. Mary Joice (nee Balmer) considered him a workaholic. She recalled, "He would carry on past midnight engrossed in affairs of Parliament, his large Diocese, Church Unity and the World Council of Churches.

"Although he took some holidays, he worked terrifically hard. For trips to London I had to accompany him to take dictation as far as Horsham. Then I got a train back to do the typing at The Palace. Fortunately, he had a strong constitution because he had little interest in food and domestic arrangements.

"The Bishop was meticulous, requiring perfection, accuracy and complete truth. People round him had to work quickly and hard because he could not wait for laggards.

"He was not all that keen on women, but was devoted to his Hetty and she to him. It was sad they had no children because he was tender hearted and fond of children. Clergy parties were held every January at The Palace and he would join in the fun.

"The Palace Grey Persian cat, Sunshine, did not find favour with him, but when somebody arrived with a French poodle which could perform tricks, he was most amused."

Former Rector of Whyke, the Rev. Richard Ratcliff, remembered Bishop Bell as a man of prime distinction, of international stature, yet fully supportive of his Diocesan clergy and careful to be in sympathy with local beliefs and consciences. A former Tangmere RAF Station Chaplain, the Rev. Leslie Foot, thought Winston Churchill misunderstood the Bishop. He differentiated between good Germans and Nazis and was against the mass bombing of cities because he could see innocent people being killed.

Bishop Bell drove himself to the end. He announced his retirement in the autumn of 1957 and moved to a new home in Canterbury, but could not give up. In April 1958 while attending discussions between Church of England and Methodist representatives in Oxford he was taken ill. He died in October that year aged 75.

Archbishop Geoffrey Fisher said at a memorial service in Chichester Cathedral that he would go down in history as one of the great glories of the Church of England.

1,500 SAW BiSHOP ENTHRONED

Chichester readily warmed to the tall and charming Dr. Roger Wilson when he arrived from Wakefield to succeed Bishop Bell. His Cathedral enthronement in April 1958 was a colourful and splendid occasion, the like of which had not been seen there for 30 years.

Ten Sussex mayors with town clerks and mace-bearers, all in full regalia, went in an impressive procession from the Assembly Rooms. Troops and airmen lined the streets. Clergy and churchwardens from all the Diocese's 400 parishes were invited so the ancient building was full to overflowing with a congregation of 1,500.

Dr. Wilson's move with his wife, Joyce, from the industrial north to rural Sussex challenged him, for he was succeeding a great man at a time of expansion and development.

From his retirement home in Wrington, Somerset, he recalled, "Wakefield was compact with a deep fellowship. By contrast, Sussex seemed more spread out, strong commuter country. The priests tended to be older and, while not lacking in faith and commitment, they were less ardent in spreading the Gospel."

It was a curious paradox, and regressive, that Sussex clergy should turn down the great possibility of Anglican-Methodist unity, for which Dr. Bell was striving at the time of his stroke. Unfortunately, Sussex, like other areas, dragged its feet. However, Bishop Wilson was able to do good ecumenical work on the continent, helping to create, and serving for 15 years on, the European Council of Churches. He retired in 1974. His wife died in 1995.

From left to right **BISHOP WILSON, DEAN HUSSEY, ROBERTSON HARE, ARCHDEACON MASON**

TWO VERY DiFFERENT DEANS

Two deans of Chichester Cathedral in the Fifties were very different characters. Senior of English deans, Arthur Duncan-Jones was authoritarian, scholarly, dogmatic and forceful, a distinguished author. Walter Hussey, his successor in 1955, was more persuasive, retiring, artistic and temperamental.

Dean Duncan-Jones was regarded as a renowned churchman and, standing 6ft. tall, he was also physically impressive. He certainly had a mind of his own, but, get to know him, and he was likable, friendly, always ready for a joke.

Altogether, he spent half a century in Holy Orders, holding the Cathedral's highest office from 1929 until his death at 75 from a heart attack in January 1955. When he celebrated the silver jubilee of his appointment in 1954 Mayor Alice Eastland gave a dinner in his honour.

Much has been written about D-J's links with Germany and a meeting with Hitler in 1933 has been recorded. But he certainly did not support Hitler or the Nazis. In fact, as a result of his 1938 book about the struggle for religious freedom in Germany, the Fuehrer named him twice in broadcasts as an enemy.

D-J spoke German and loved pre-Hitler Germany. He and his wife went there for their honeymoon and, interested in the history and culture, spent many family holidays in the country. Knowing good German people, they were upset by the terrible events and were concerned for religious freedom.

For several years, the last in 1954, the Dean led the great Festival of Remembrance at the Royal Albert Hall.

Few 20th century deans did as much as he for the Cathedral. He restored the fabric, arranged worship on a more stately and splendid scale and made it a real Mother Church of the Diocese.

His noted book, 'The Chichester Customary,' resulting from many years study of church rites, became known throughout the Anglican world. He loved music and art and, through regular contact with the organists, transformed the Cathedral music. End-of-term services for local school children were his idea and he also started the Epiphany Service.

Interested in Chichester's history and welfare, he became chairman of the Civic Society, attended music recitals and Historical Association lectures and joined the Rotary Club.

Life at the 18-room Deanery was not quiet and cloistered, for there were six sons and two daughters, a busy church and social life and books to be written.

"Father was tough with us, at times impatient ," recalled a daughter, Mrs. Ursula Baily. "I regarded him with awe, but his huge sense of humour was a saving grace. He worked tremendously hard and was often away for Church Assembly and World Council of Churches work.

"At Christmas we had wonderful family parties. Mother was a lovely woman and all the family adored her. She wrote family biographies, fairy tales and books about St. Richard and St. Francis and the story of Christendom. In the early years she was also father's secretary. Yet she still managed to write twice a week to absent children."

Mrs. Duncan-Jones died in 1966.

ARTiSTiC DEAN - A PiONEER

Art loving Walter Hussey pioneered the Church's use of contemporary art and left his own remarkable collection of 130-140 works for showing in Pallant House Gallery.

Recalling the Dean's early interest, the Gallery's curator, David Coke, said, "He started in a small way and, never rich, he had to be astute. He also had a remarkable ability to spot real talent before an artist became well known.

"He was an unassuming and very approachable man, thoughtful, intelligent and sensitive. Yet, he could be determined if he wanted something badly. Because of his rather introverted nature he has never been given the credit he deserves for the vital part he played in the 20th century renaissance of real church art.

"Chichester must be unique among English cathedrals for being so well-endowed with high quality art of our own century. Deans tend, naturally, to be more interested in liturgy and music than visual art. Dean Hussey saw them as an integral part of church worship."

Dean Hussey's secretary, Mrs. Hilary Bryan-Brown, found him a stimulating and rewarding person to work for during the nine years she was with him, although he could be temperamental.

"He was an intensely private man, lonely, retiring and shy, but he was a wonderful raconteur, very observant. People thought him remote, but he had much humour. You had to get to know him. He fascinated me with his wide interest in all aspects of the arts and we used to talk endlessly about people and music, ideas for things for the Cathedral and his collection of paintings.

"When he acquired something new he would put it where he could see it from his desk and just savour it through the day. Often it was weeks before he would hang it properly. I remember, particularly, an eagle's head by Romano. We just used to gaze at it. I loved working in such a rarefied atmosphere.

"I was involved because I dealt with the correspondence and he talked to me about adornments for the Cathedral. Walter was indefatigable in his pursuit of 'ideas for the Cathedral.' "

SAD SHOP CLOSURES

Family owned city centre shops were regrettably disappearing during the decade and one of the first to go was Harris and Hall, 150-year-old grocers and wine merchants right by the Cross in East Street. War-time rationing affected trade badly and, although tall, cricket loving Bill Hall, a Sussex Yeomanry sergeant, and the half-a-dozen staff worked hard, it never recovered sufficiently and closed in 1951. (Now Birthdays, a card shop).

Mr. Hall's grandfather started the old fashioned business and farmers and country houses taking bulk orders were good customers. Members of the family were killed by the German bomb which hit St. Martin's.

BILL HALL

BUNN'S BANANAS

George Bunn's Orchard Stores on the East Street-Baffins Lane corner was more than a handy vegetable and fruit shop. In the cellar was a gas heater for ripening thousands of bananas sent by train from Southampton Docks for sale to the trade.

It was a wholesale as well as retail business, supplying schools, hospitals and caterers. Mr. Bunn closed down in the early Sixties to help with the large family White Horse Caravan business at Selsey. His younger brother, Douglas Bunn, founded the Hickstead show jumping arena.

A.& N. BOUGHT MORANTS

Army and Navy Stores came to Chichester in 1955 when a City benefactor, Edgar Tozer, Deputy Mayor in 1956, sold his large departmental store of Morants. Three months of negotiations ensured the 80 staff would be kept on without change.

During the decade the former Oliver Whitby School, which closed in 1950, and the neighbouring Tower Cafe were taken over and the old Southdown bus depot became the shoe department.

An unassuming, generous man, Mr. Tozer bought an empty bungalow and garden from the Methodist Church in the Hornet for pensioners. Old folks' champions, Charles and Marjorie Newell, led successful efforts to turn this into a rest room and canteen, the forerunner of the Newell Centre. The benefactor's name is commemorated in Tozer Way.

JAY'S £46,000 SALE TO TESCO

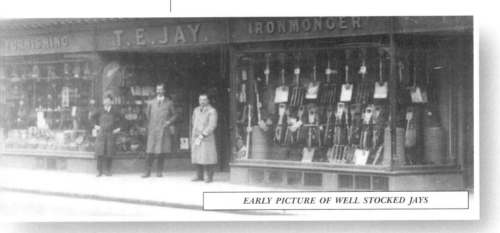

EARLY PICTURE OF WELL STOCKED JAYS

East Street ironmonger Tom Jay, magistrate, Rotarian and Royal Sussex Regiment Captain, got his own back on planners who refused him permission for a shopping mall. Knowing they did not want supermarkets, he deliberately sold his century old business in 1959 to Tesco. He got £46,000 for a site that must now be worth a million.

"Father had a fit of pique," recalled son, Thomas Jay. "He decided to give up ironmongery and go to the family farm in Herefordshire. The shop was large, going back to the Butter Market, and he thought it would make an ideal shopping mall. But the planners did not agree, so, knowing they did not like supermarkets, because the International Stores (now Superdrug) had been converted to one, he sold to Tesco. He was that sort of man."

Heated only by paraffin stoves, Jays was a remarkable shop, an Aladdin's Cave, full of the most varied stock, worth thousands of pounds. Bargain hunters flocked in for the closing sale and the first morning realised £500.

GREAT GALA DAYS

Gala Day sadly faded away in the Nineties, but in the Fifties, with community spirit at its strongest, the City looked forward to a great family day out. Top bands marched through the crowded streets, 20,000 cornflowers were grown for an emblem, attractions filled Priory Park and there was a mile-long carnival procession.

Money flowed in all day, although the idea of Chichester Combined Charities was not just to help charity but give the City a holiday. With the blessing of perfect weather the first Gala in July 1955 was a great success, raising £1,250.

Mayor Leslie Evershed-Martin, the originator, was thrilled because a lot of pleasure was provided and it was not necessary to touch the Council's £500 guarantee against loss. Thirty floats were entered for the carnival procession and that was not the end of the day. At dusk there was a torchlight procession led by two bands and a finale by the Royal Marines Band performing Beat the Retreat and Sunset Ceremony.

Chosen as the first Miss Gala in 1957 was brunette Brenda Davis, a married shop assistant and former Sunday School teacher. She was crowned by racing driver Jack Fairman at the Gaumont, where selection was by audience applause.

Bikinis were out for the competition. Measuring vital statistics would not be proper for a nice place like Chichester, ruled the organiser, Jack Miller, who ran the Gala funfair and then became Gala Secretary, assisted by wife Mollie.

GOODWOOD'S TWO GREAT SPORTS

Goodwood Races were even more glorious in the Fifties when Royalty graced the picturesque course. While below the Downs, in days when there were no noise protests, racing drivers like Stirling Moss, Reg Parnell and Graham Hill created a great motor sport era on the old Westhampnett airfield.

The Queen's visit in her accession year, 1952, was the first by a Sovereign since her grandfather, King George V, attended in 1928.

With the course at its best, buildings newly painted, the setting was glorious, a garden party plus racing, as King Edward V11 would have remarked. Attendance for that opening day was 51,800.

Shortly before the Queen's arrival at Goodwood House in 1955 there was a power cut. An underground cable fault hit the area, including local villages. In 1957 the Queen became the season's most successful owner when her filly, Almeria, won the Bentinck Stakes. The £1,153 success brought her prize money to £41,034.

Princess Margaret made informal visits in 1949, 50 and 51, staying at the Graffham home of the Hon. Mrs. Agar.

Chichester was practically empty on Thursday afternoons during race week. Shops closed as the City went racing. The races were televised for the first time in 1951.

Friendly rivalry on the motor circuit thrilled thousands, the scenes and smell reviving memories of pre-war Brooklands. Petrol rationing went on until 1950, but for the first race in 1948 there were 15,000 spectators. Parked cars littered the roads.

The late Duke of Richmond and Gordon, a leading enthusiast of the sport, became President of the British Automobile Racing Club, which organised the events. He saw Goodwood playing its part in achieving world supremacy for British cars and top drivers took part. History was made in 1951 by a nine hour race, finishing at midnight.

MiSERLY JEWELLERS LEFT A MiLLiON

Eccentric jewellers Ronnie Allen and sister Maisie led penny pinching Victorian lives at the extraordinary South Street shop (now Rowlands and Past Times), which they inherited in 1958. They never went on holiday and after a rare day out would come back and work until late.

Staff were given the minimum of wages, none at all if they were sick, and they were even expected to go halves on tips. Visitors were not welcome at their Westgate home. It was untidy, overrun with cats, reportedly numbering 30.

Yet the Allens owned many shops and houses. When a safe, stolen in a raid on their home, was discovered in Hambrook Pit it was found to contain the deeds of a large part of South Street and Cooper Street, four houses in Orchard Avenue, property in West Street and Westgate and houses in Bognor Road, Green Lane, Summersdale and Selsey.

In their wills they left £1.27 million, a lot to St. Paul's Church and the RNLI.

Keith Masters, now Cathedral Sacristan, who started at the shop in 1950 as an apprentice, described the Allens as eccentric, very Victorian, dedicated to work. "Ronnie had the gift of the gab, walking around whistling unmelodiously, but he never really did any work. He shook hands with every caller and sealed packages with wax from a gas flame. When petrol was rationed he bought cans of lighter fuel to keep his old Rover going.

"His sister was the business partner. When I asked for a second week's holiday I was told I could have it but without pay. "

Burgled several times, the shop looked a muddle, dimly lit and sparsely heated with just a one bar electric fire for seven workshop staff. All the jewellery could not be displayed and was stuffed into shoe boxes, apparently never sold. In latter years the shop shutters remained down and it was suggested the place was closed for health or safety reasons.

Ronnie and Maisie ended life in their 80s, she dying three months after him in 1993. Their very astute father, Charlie Allen, Mayor of the City, who started the business, died in 1958 aged 86. Workshop foreman, Harold Smith, described him as a grand old man, very clever at his job.

SOCIAL LIFE HIT

Social organisations were hit by the sudden closure of the 200-year-old Assembly Rooms for safety reasons in December 1951 and the sale of Laurie Kimbell's restaurant and confectionery business, nearly opposite, in September 1954.

Refurbishments at the Assembly Rooms cost approaching £17,000, nearly double the estimate, and took until 1953. Although it was a worthwhile job, there were still problems for some organisations and, with seating limited to 250, a number found difficulty in covering costs.

Customers familiar with Kimbell's fine hall, staircase and balcony keenly felt the loss of the premises. It was an ideal setting for dances and civic dinners. John Perring's furniture shop moved in.

NEW CARS FOR £500

Walking through the pedestrian precincts in the Nineties it is difficult to picture half-a-dozen garages practically within sight of the Cross. Yet, early in the decade, owners were selling petrol for 3s-4s. a gallon and new cars for £500, if they could get them.

And that was the problem because cars were in short supply and there was a waiting list of 4,000 customers. Dealers had to put up with what they got from factories and a dealer's quota might be only six Morris Minors in two months. Colour could not be guaranteed.

There were virtually no foreign cars and spares were also difficult to obtain. In 1956, fuel rationing caused by the Suez crisis created further difficulties.

General manager John Lanham found good customer loyalty at Wadhams, Southgate. Businesses were lost in the redevelopment of that area, now the site of the JobCentre, City Gates and Avenue de Chartres, which cut across Westgate Fields, where the £620,000 College was built.

SOUTHGATE

Rowes Garage moved from premises now occupied by Kwik-Fit to what used to be a sheep grazing field. Robert Knight, who rose from tractor salesman to company chairman, recalled the heavy agricultural bias of the profitable business. "Long before it became fashionable, we had an apprenticeship scheme, with day release facilities, and built up a loyal bunch of long serving workers."

THE HORNET

17

SOUTH STREET

Fields, South Street (now M.W., Tandy and Music and Video Club), dealt in Austins and manager Roger Winsor remembered selling A30s for about £500. The business did well and expanded, setting up a depot on the industrial estate.

EAST STREET

For 6d. a day motorists could park in a yard beside Adcocks, Rootes Group agents in East Street. The garage was run by Cecil 'Gig' Herniman, who was prominent as a former mayor and member of three local councils. Among businesses now in the area are Sofa Workshop, Snips and Amoeba Jewellers, with the Social Security offices above. Northgate Priory Lanes shopping arcade was the site of a garage run by Thomas Reed, who moved from a building next to the Prebendal School.

Masons, run by City Alderman Alan Mason, was converted to Waitrose (now Argos and neighbours). Pope's Garage, Northgate, was owned by Bill Pope, who became Mayor of Chichester.

CROSS-CHANNEL TWiNS

The Entente Cordiale was at its most cordial when Chichester twinned with the French city of Chartres.

Hundreds of young people from the two Cathedral cities have happy memories of annual exchange visits and many organisations enjoy lasting links.

"There was great enthusiasm for the Twinning," recalled long serving councillor Mrs. Kathleen Smith, who was involved in the early arrangements. "Every year about 50 children have enjoyed exchange holidays. When Tom Siggs went over as Mayor we discussed how we could make Chartres part of Chichester and we thought of calling the new road leading from Southgate, Avenue de Chartres."

The 1958 Mayor and Mayoress, Charles and Marjorie Newell, were among a party which went to Chartres to make the first arrangements. Representatives of the two cities formally agreed to unite at a Chichester council chamber meeting in February 1959.

The Newells named their daughter, Soline, and wedding bells for Nigel and Martine Purchase was another happy result of the twinning.

PURCHASE'S LiQUOR PRiCES

In 1951 Scotch Whisky and champagne were well under £2 a bottle and sherry less than £1 a bottle at specialist wine merchants, Arthur Purchase and Son, North Street. George Purchase and son Russell, who was a good Mayor of Chichester, supplied fine wines, spirits and ales to Goodwood, Stansted and other big country houses.

Then 70 per cent of their trade was retail, a totally different proportion compared with today's supermarket dominated conditions. The shop has been handed down from father to son through six generations since 1780, reputedly the oldest such business in the country. It was moved from nextdoor (now Laura Ashley) in 1956.

Russell Purchase, who grew a beard for the new Elizabethan age following the Queen's accession, imparted his knowledge of the trade with typical sophistication when he entertained 100 members of the Connoisseurs' Society to a novel candlelit Burgundy wine tasting evening in the Assembly Rooms in 1954.

BULLDOG SHiRTS SHOP

South Street gents outfitters Turnbull (now TSB) was run by ex-City Mayor George Turnbull and later his son, Leslie. Their speciality was grey and rough looking Bulldog shirts worn by workmen. These contrasted sharply with the more select Jaegar woollies.

SHEET MUSiC 1s.

Austin Storrys, North Street (Fosters), was the only shop for musicians wanting sheet music, instruments and accessories. Well-stocked, it was run by Ed Munt, a good violinist, who played in local orchestras.

Piano teacher Joyce Foote recalled days when sheet music cost 1s. "My father bought our first baby grand at Storry's for 60 guineas. I started giving lessons to pay the money back."

*WORKMEN LAYING A ZEBRA PEDESTRIAN CROSSING OUTSIDE WILF BARTHOLOMEW'S TOBACCONISTS
AND S.J. LINKINS' SPORT SHOP, SOUTH STREET, IN JANUARY 1952.
PRE-STRESSED CONCRETE SLABS WERE USED FOR A ROAD RESEARCH LABORATORY EXPERIMENT.*

*FROM SHEET MUSIC TO PIANOS AND TVS, STORRYS OFFERED A
COMPLETE RANGE OF HOME ENTERTAINMENT FACILITIES.*

*LATEST FASHIONS WERE AVAILABLE AT MORANTS.
EDGAR TOZER SOLD THE LARGE STORE TO A & N IN 1955.*

TRAVELLING TOWARDS THE CROSS ALONG SOUTH STREET, A MORRIS MINOR HAS PASSED: SYKES AND SON (DRAPERS); F.M. BARBER LTD (FISH, POULTRY AND GAME), RUN BY COUSINS FRED AND TED BARBER; LONDON CENTRAL MEAT COMPANY, MANAGER MR. JOCELYN; GRIFFITH BROTHERS (GENTS OUTFITTERS), MANAGER BILL PRESTRIDGE; SHIPPAMS (GROCERS); RUSSELL AND BROMLEY LTD (SHOES); W.H. BARRETT (BOOKSELLER, STATIONER AND NEWSAGENT).

BREACH'S WINE AND SPIRIT SHOP ON THE EAST STREET - NORTH PALLANT CORNER (NOW ALEXON). THERE WAS A TUDOR CAFE IN EAST STREET AND TOWER CAFE IN WEST STREET, RUN BY THE SMITH BROTHERS. WHEN MORANTS (NOW ARMY AND NAVY) BOUGHT THE TOWER CAFE FOR ITS OWN CAFE A. SMITH CONCENTRATED HIS BUSINESS ON THE TUDOR CAFE. IN THE NORTH PALLANT DOORWAY BEHIND BREACH'S COULD BE FOUND THE OFTEN UNNOTICED RIFLEMAN PUB, USED BY BUSINESSMEN.

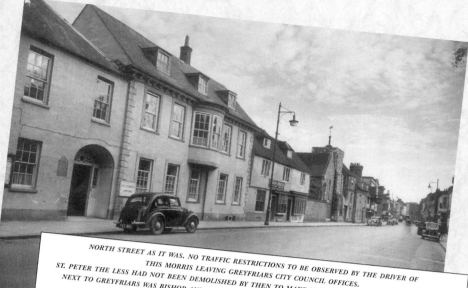

NORTH STREET AS IT WAS. NO TRAFFIC RESTRICTIONS TO BE OBSERVED BY THE DRIVER OF THIS MORRIS LEAVING GREYFRIARS CITY COUNCIL OFFICES.
ST. PETER THE LESS HAD NOT BEEN DEMOLISHED BY THEN TO MAKE WAY FOR THE NEW ROAD, ST. PETERS.
NEXT TO GREYFRIARS WAS BISHOP AND BROOKE LTD., YEAST MANUFACTURERS, AND VECK FIRE PLACES,
LATER DAVID COVER, FIRE PLACE SPECIALISTS.
UNALTERED TODAY, THIS IS ONE OF THE OLDEST FRONTAGES IN TOWN, NOW OCCUPIED
BY MRS. ELIZABETH TURNER FOR LADIES' FASHIONS AND BY HER SON, MARCO TURNER, FOR MEN'S WEAR.

CYCLES AND PEDESTRIANS MAKE NORTH STREET LOOK BUSY OUTSIDE SIDNEY BASTOW (CHEMISTS),
WOOLWORTH'S AND ANDREWS (CYCLES). OPPOSITE IS THE LARGE DRAPERS, GEERINGS,
AND FURTHER ALONG THE ASSEMBLY ROOMS.

FIFTIES' ATMOSPHERE IS PROVIDED BY THESE CINEMA AND GARAGE ADVERTISEMENTS.

WESTGATE BOTTLENECK - BUILDINGS WERE BULLDOZED FOR THE WESTGATE ROUNDABOUT

FiSHMONGERS WERE CAUGHT

Price controls, restricted supplies and rising rents created problems for fishmongers. Dick Kimbell, who ran Byerleys, South Street, which was started by his great grandfather in 1872, recalled, "We did not know what the 5.30 am fish train was going to bring every morning from Grimsby or Hull.

"Although fish was cheaper than meat, the price we could charge was fixed by the Ministry. In addition, the Dean and Chapter made big increases in rents. People don't realise now the difficulties of life in the Fifties."

iRONMONGER'S NiGHTMARE

Bob Pine's difficulties at his Eastgate Square ironmongery and Sub-Post Office, which he ran for half a century, employing 30 staff, led him to become a strong critic of local planning.

"After a lot of delay I was allowed to knock down three of five tiny cottages in order to build a two-storey extension, but it was not what I wanted. A lot of shopkeepers experienced difficulties over extensions, refurbishments, frontages and signs. They found the regulations a nightmare."

As chairman of the Chamber of Commerce, Mr. Pine presided over a big meeting to challenge what was considered to be a dictatorial attitude. He thought that, eventually, some sanity was achieved.

BREWERS CUT FOR PUBS

Two hundred staff pondered their fate when they heard that Richard Henty, their Old Etonian boss at Henty and Constable Brewery, had died of a heart attack on the Queen Mary in February 1954. They did not know that the future of 250 pubs and hotels in Sussex and Hampshire was going to be decided by cutting cards. Westgate Brewery, now recognisable only by the names of housing estate roads, Henty Gardens and The Maltings, had to go to meet death duties. Friary and Watney divided the pubs between them at the Unicorn.

Licensee and historian Mervyn Cutten said it was done by mutual agreement and Doug Harcourt, who, as licensee, provided lunch, added, "They chose the pubs alternately. Henty and Constable was a tip-top brewery and I was sorry to see it go. They used to send a collector round for the rent and preferred payment by cash."

THE FLEECE INN

With his wife, Kay, Mr. Harcourt, a Fleet Air Arm petty officer and RAF Squadron Leader, was host for many organisations at the Unicorn until 1960 when Watney decided it was no longer viable. It had been Tangmere airmen's drinking home in the Forties and a social centre in the Fifties. A meal there cost 4s.6d.

Business-like, but happy and charming, Mr. Henty took personal interest in licensees' welfare and they liked him. Only 50 when he died, he did much to steer in the NHS in Chichester.

Brewery staff were allowed to drink two milk bottles of beer a day. Ron McCormack recalled, "There were three vats producing a lot of really good quality beer. Social and sporting clubs made it a very happy place to work."

PUB SHORTS

THE MITRE, opened in 1957, the first new pub for nearly 80 years. It was built to serve residents from the 500 houses at Parklands.

CHRIS WALKER, the Ship Inn, Tower Street, was secretary of the Licensed Victuallers' Association until 1958 when he retired aged 79, to be succeeded by Fred Loveland, Rainbow Inn.

THE STAR, which was lost in the Somerstown slum clearance, was crowded with Festival Theatre stars. Mine hosts, Godfrey and Sylvia Yockney, used to order whisky, gin and rum for 18p a gallon. Their beer was 4d. a pint.

NURSERY ARMS, a working class pub in Orchard Street (now flats), ran a tontine which paid out £1,000 at Christmas. Tom and Lucy Rossiter were doing well until double yellow lines spoiled trade.

THE OLD CROSS, North Street, run by Mr. and Mrs. Bates, was popular with organisations and city councillors. When George and Laura Allouis moved in from their West End restaurant they built up a great custom with Festival Theatre stars.

1951 'STREET' STAR

Coronation Street star Peter Baldwin, a former Chichester High School boy, was on stage at the Bishop's Palace in July 1951 for the memorable Festival of Britain play, The Boy with a cart,' by Christopher Fry. His portrayal of 'Tawn' showed he was obviously a budding professional.

Between 70 and 80 local amateurs took part in the faultless production by Hugh Manning of BBC and Bristol Old Vic fame.

CHARGE FOR QUALiTY

Charge and Co., on a City Cross corner (now Midland Bank), was a good quality drapery and ladies' fashion house, run by the Charge family for two centuries, latterly by Peter Charge.

There was nearly two dozen staff. Miss Joan Marsh, who started as a £1 a month apprentice, remembered, "Stockings cost 1s.11d. and you could get gloves from 4s.11d. Hats were a speciality, popular for Goodwood Races. Patterns and materials for dressmaking were also a good line."

The popular Peter Charge and his twin, Paul, were born on the premises. Peter succeeded his mother and aunt in 1936 and was the last of the family. After he retired in 1968 the building was sold to the Bank for £60, 000.

DRAPER'S HARD SLOG

Like other shopkeepers, Peter Sykes in his century old South Street drapery struggled against rising rents, shortages and competition. "However, Chichester was a happy place to trade," he recalled. "Although there were about nine similar businesses, rivalry was friendly."

Sykes employed about 17 staff and was known as 'The house for piece goods,' offering value and variety. Utility lingerie crepe was 6s.1d. a yard, taffeta 3s.6d. a yard, hats 5s. to 10s., corsets 10s., ankle socks 2s.3d. a pair and frocks from 25s. Not many shops sold ready-made clothing. Women bought patterns and took pleasure in making their own dresses.

GEERiNGS' CASH RAiLWAY

A cash railway was an intriguing feature in the old fashioned North Street drapers, Geerings (now Between the Lines and Robert Dyas). Money and receipts were propelled, noisily, along overhead wires to a central cash desk.

Desmond Cockayne, Selsey Lifeboat Secretary. inherited the system when he bought the store from Mr. Geering in 1950-51. Mrs. Margaret Cockayne (widow) remembered it as a large, very successful store, employing 30. "Things were often priced to the last farthing. Because the rates went sky high we sold up and bought a shop at Littlehampton. Chichester missed the shop badly when it closed."

BARLEY FOR THE BREWERS

The Corn Exchange (now John Wiley and Sons) was an important centre because the prime agricultural land around Chichester produced fine quality wheat, oats and barley. Feed for the many horses, and malt and hops for brewing, were stable commodities.

Jack Bartholomew, chairman of the century old agricultural merchants, Bartholomews Ltd., employing 160, recalled, "It was a meeting place for farmers to sell grain to corn merchants, who, in turn, sold to millers and maltsers. Deals were done on hand shakes at stands which were rather like school desks."

Bartholomews used to operate from Northgate, the building still identifiable by the preserved frontage and original lettering. There was also a shop at 12 North Street (now Woolworths), selling feeds, seeds and fertilisers. Most flower seeds were 4d. a packet.

Changes in farming resulted in the Corn Exchange's decline and now most crops are grown under contract.

26 PAPER BOYS AT FiELDERS

PETER FIELDER

Peter Fielder, keen footballer, cricketer and archer, at the East Street newsagents, tobacconists and confectioners, Fielder and Son, (now Roco) where 10 Woodbines cost 1s.6d. and Mars bars 2d. There were 26 paper boys making deliveries in days when a daily paper cost 1d. or 2d.

"It was a very busy shop," remembered Mrs. Pat Fielder (widow). "Being open from 6am to 6pm we had hundreds of customers a day and takings came to £1,000 a week. Accounts took a lot of time and rising council rates were a problem."

A wide range of sweets had to be weighed individually from large glass jars on the shelves. Wrapped boiled sweets were 10p. a quarter, Maltesers 1s.6d. a box, chocolate bars 2d. to 4d. and Pinks soft drinks 6d. a bottle.

As many people smoked - there were no health warnings then - cigarettes formed a big part of the trade. Those wanting to appear elite smoked Du Maurier. Roy Fielder (brother) died suddenly aged 47 on the day the shop closed, New Year's Eve 1971, and it was sold for £125,000.

JARS BY THE MiLLiON

Shippams workers at a 1955 house-warming to mark an extension of the East Walls factory. In front, left to right, are Annabella Hammond, Mrs. White, Joan Baldwin and George Ide.

The two centuries old firm enjoyed considerable growth, doubling its workforce to 679 by 1959 and doubling its profits. "We introduced new varieties and made big progress which meant much reconstruction," recalled Jim Shippam, the last of the family to be in charge. "It was a decade of significant expansion."

The number of jars of paste sold increased during the Fifties from 22 million to 43 million. Sales amounting to £630,000 in 1950 were £2.1m. in 1959.

Following a bad fishing season in 1954, the Chichester Lass was commissioned to lead research into radar for locating pilchard shoals. A small factory was established at Newlyn. The only curtailment was the sale of the South Street shop (now Millets), which was popular for Shippams meat pies and sausages.

DONNiNGTON HOME, A FiRST

Mr. Percie Shippam (centre) with those who helped push forward the provision of Chichester Eventide Association's Donnington home, the first such residence for the elderly. The £6,500 house was given by Mr. Shippam in 1950 in memory of his wife, Rose. Two or three years fund raising and hard work by volunteers made the £12,000 project possible. When the first 14 semi-infirm residents moved in during January 1952 figures showed it would be self-supporting once the remaining £3,500 worth of liabilities had been cleared. Miss M. Price (right) was the first matron.

BUSY MARKET DAYS

AUCTIONEER HENRY ADAMS

Hundreds of cattle, pigs and sheep filled the pens in the heyday of Chichester Cattle Market. Farmers' fears in the Fifties were not about BSE but foot and mouth disease, swine fever and fowl pest. The country came to town on Wednesdays, creating a focal point of trade, a vital part of the City's prosperity for generations.

Wagon loads of cattle arrived by rail, some herded bellowing through the streets, others kept temporarily on Westgate Fields and at Summersdale. Helping to increase trade during the decade was the welcome return of fatstock auctioneering.

In 1952 the City Council spent £15,000 on improvements to make it one of the best attested markets in the south. Trade built up and remained good for 20 years. Average weekly numbers going under the hammer were 300 store and dairy cattle, 150 calves and 200 sheep, mostly Southdown. Sometimes every pen was full.

Brothers Pat and Dan Stride, sons of war-time Mayor Walter Stride, carried on the 100-year-old firm of Stride and Son. They auctioned cattle and sheep, while Wyatt and Son auctioned pigs, poultry, produce and dead stock. Auctioneers included Pat Stride, John Willis, Ted Cattermole, Henry Adams, John Gates, Dick Keating and Michael Roberts.

Auctioneers' clerks Norman Mills, Guy Walker, Jack Jupp, Bill Ridgely, Norman Adams, Fred Streatfield and Dick Blackman, booked in animals from 7am and ensured the 160-170 vendors got their cheques Friday mornings.

Changes in farming, doubts about the market's future and competition from other markets began to affect trade. It ended on October 24 1990 and then demolition men began the £1m. scheme to sweep away all traces of the enterprise for a car park.

AUCTIONEER PAT STRIDE

Veteran farmer **Tom Rusbridge** criticised the Council for acting against farmers' interests and hastening the end. "They let in market traders, completely forgetting the City's prosperity was founded on Southdown Sheep, which provided the highest quality wool for wool stapler Ebenezer Prior. Devon cattle and Southdown sheep were giving traditional butchers their best meat."

COLOURFUL MARKET CHARACTERS

JOHN WILLIS looked and sounded every bit an auctioneer, his voice booming across the pens from under one of his eight Utah Stetsons. With lively wit and engaging patter from the rostrum he coaxed farmers into bidding to the limit. His widow, Jean, was impressed by his professionalism as well as his great fun, for he was one of the most knowledgeable and best qualified men. In the mid-Fifties he made it his personal business to build up trade, persuading farmers and dealers to come to Chichester. Tenants had in him a champion. He did battle for them over rents and other problems.

ADA SMITH organised and numbered cattle, working happily with the beasts for 61 years. Once she was gored by a heifer and suffered a broken finger as other cows clambered over her. She could not find out who owned the heifers, but a £10 cheque was later put through her letterbox.

TED GOBY, cattle drover, was often the worse for drink and sometimes in court. Known as the One Armed Bandit because of an arm deformity, he could be seen around the town taunting the police.

EDGAR BANKS, second hand dealer, was well known for the Aladdin's Cave business he ran from old sheds.

ROTTiNG STATiON RE-BUiLT

Long awaited reconstructions at the archaic Railway Station, where 80 staff were seeing over 100 trains a day safely through, began at last in 1957. It was notorious as the worst station in the south, dinghy, undecorated, even rotting, lit only by gas.

All the buildings were systematically replaced to provide the most up-to-date facilities, dominated by an attractive booking hall. The two-year operation, carried out mainly at night, was part of a £1.2m. countrywide modernisation.

Although the footbridge and signal box were painted in 1953, no outside decorating had been done for 35 years because reconstruction was always in the offing. Councillors protested in vain about the conditions.

Station clerk Phil Norrell, described it as a dinghy dump. Everything had to be rebuilt. Passenger booking clerk Alec Smith recalled the dilapidated Victorian buildings and the trying working conditions. "It was difficult to cope in the booking office, trying to sell tickets, answering inquiries and making up the few pounds a week wages for staff."

COMMUTERS travelled by green £19.6s.6d. season tickets on the 7am or 7.50 am to London. A queue stretched from the pavement for the popular 8.54 am London day excursion (13s.6d) and for the Isle of Wight.

HOURLY STOPPING TRAIN IN THE BAY

Eight hundred day return tickets to Fratton (2s.11d.) were sold for a Pompey home match. Workmen paid 1s.9d. for a grey return ticket to Portsmouth. There was an evening excursion to Portsmouth, also costing 1s.9d., and a half-day excursion to London for 10s.6d.

Bags of mail were handled, boxes of fish were delivered and half-a-dozen coal merchants operated from the large, busy goods yard weighing supplies hauled from collieries.

STATION CHARACTERS

ALF HALL, ticket collector, could be mistaken for the station master as he strutted around looking smart in a well pressed uniform, sporting a button hole.

TITCH HURREN, porter, was well known for dressing up as a clown for charity events. During the flood disaster appeals of 1952 he went round with a donkey cart and collected £26.

BEN IDE picked up boxes of fish from the 5.30am fish train for delivery to fishmongers on his large barrow.

27 BUSES AN HOUR

Motorists as well as passengers benefited when the new Bus Station opened in September 1956 because traffic congestion round the old West Street premises and the Cross was relieved and Southdown could run 19 services with 27 buses an hour over a large part of West Sussex.

Citizens were pleased to see the Southgate area cleared up. The old police station and derelict houses and gardens had been an eyesore for 15 years.

Negotiations over Southdown's biggest project, the best bus station in the south, took years. The City Council bought the site in 1950 for £8,590 and agreement was reached for Southdown to rent it for 99 years at £450 a year. The company also bought the area across Basin Road for a workshop and garage to take 60-70 buses.

No 11 West Street (now a shoe shop), which had been the bus station for 25-30 years, was sold and the garage at Northgate was bought by the Post Office.

Drivers had to turn their buses by backing out of Tower Street. Operating from a sentry box, Bob Mayne blew a whistle when the way was clear.

Long serving busman Ron Rines remembered how 25 staff were crammed into half-a-dozen rooms. "It really was primitive. The cashier's office was an old greenhouse at the back and the canteen was a cow stall. In contrast, the Southate premises were a palace."

SOUTHDOWN No.66 IN NORTH STREET

FARES look low today and they did not go up much: Chichester-Selsey and Chichester-Bognor Regis 1s. (1s.6d. return), Lavant 4d., Fishbourne Post Office 2d., Old Bosham 6d.

PAY was 2s.5d. an hour for drivers and 2s.4d. for conductors, but there was overtime. The men looked smart in peaked caps and uniforms. From May 1 to September 30 a white cap cover was compulsory.

LAST BUSES were provided to take people home from cinemas. Between 10pm and 10.23pm on Saturday nights there were 23 departures from West Street. As passengers numbered hundreds three buses were kept as reliefs because there were queues for most routes.

BUS SHELTER SAGA- Incredibly, long suffering passengers had to wait nearly three years, until the end of the decade, for a bus shelter in West Street. Concerned about appearances, councillors went to the extent in 1957 of calling in top architect Basil Spence for advice. They even thought of putting a modern structure between the Bell Tower buttresses. Eventually, a special bus shelter committee with authority to spend £200 found a site on part of the garden in front of the Cathedral.

WHEN THE MEN OF SUSSEX MARCHED

The Fifties were momentous years for the Royal Sussex Regiment, starting with the presentation of the Freedom of Chichester on June 30 1951. But in the next decade the famous fighting unit was consigned to history by savage defence cuts.

To general regret, proud county regiments were amalgamated for the Sixties' New Army and the Royal Sussex became part of the Home Counties Brigade and, later, the Queen's Regiment.

The Barracks was given its Roussillon name by the Duke of Norfolk in 1959 before an immense crowd watching the last celebrations there to mark the victorious Battle of Quebec 200 years earlier.

Royal Military Police men and women moved from Woking in 1963 to become a new source of civic attention and thousands of pounds were spent on updating. Ironically, an oak tree planted in 1960 at the end of the County Regiment's 87 years' occupation failed to take root.

While the 850-strong 1st. Battalion spent time abroad during the Fifties, the Barracks was a hive of activity. Batches of National Servicemen were given six weeks basic training there and wooden quarters going back to the Napoleonic Wars were replaced.

C.O. 1951-53 Major John Ainsworth, a World War 11 German POW: "The Barracks contained a big gym', officers' and men's' quarters and messes. It was not only a regimental depot, but a training base. We also administered the infantry clerks training course."

Enacted with full pageantry and splendour, the Freedom ceremony was held during the Festival of Britain, two days after the Regiment's 250th birthday. In Priory Park 250 men paraded for inspection by Mayor Russell Purchase and the Duke of Norfolk, both of whom served in the Regiment.

Centrepiece of the occasion was the presentation of a handsome silver Altar Cross, the gift of the City for St. George's Chapel in the Cathedral. This was received by the Colonel of the Regiment, Brigadier Frank Foster, and dedicated by Bishop Bell during a Cathedral service.

MAJOR JOHN AINSWORTH

OYAL SUSSEX MARCH PAST

There followed a civic lunch in Kimbells and, rounding off the day, was an all-ranks dance at the Barracks. From dusk to midnight the Sussex Yeomanry floodlit the Cathedral spire.

The Regiment received the Freedom of other county towns and another source of pride was the appointment in 1953 of Queen Juliana of the Netherlands as Colonel-in-Chief, thus renewing a 250-year-old link with the House of Orange.

NATIONAL SERVICE continued until 1962 and recruits found life tough at the Barracks. "We instilled in them the need for strict discipline," recalled John White, who spent 24 years in the Army and is secretary of Chichester and District Branch of the Royal Sussex Regimental Association. "There had to be an immediate response to orders.

"Esprit-de-corps was magnificent. Our's was the best of the county regiments and we were very sorry to lose our identity, although in the Queen's Regiment we were called the 3rd. Battalion (Royal Sussex)".

'**BOLO**' was the nickname of perhaps the most notable and charismatic Royal Sussex officer - General Sir Lashmer Whistler, a former C.O. of the Barracks. In World War 11 Monty gave him command of the famous 3rd Division, which was in the thick of fighting from Normandy to the Baltic. Ex-City Mayor Thomas Siggs, President of the Association: "The General encouraged me to join up. When he saw me later on guard duty in Palestine he got me released to do some exhibition boxing."

FiGHTERS LEAVE TANGMERE

Tangmere RAF Station's illustrious role as a top fighter base ended in June 1958 with an historic parade attended by famous war-time pilots. But though squadrons were disbanded, the men were transferred to other units and their standards handed over, so tradition continued. They were sorry to go because Tangmere was always a favourite posting.

Jet-age Hunters and Meteors shattered Chichester's peace as they roared off from the airfield. Their departure meant 90 civilian staff, many from Chichester, worried about their future. However, it was not the end of the base where the best known pilot of all, Douglas Bader, once served. Signals Command moved in with Varsities and Canberras for radar and calibration work. The 1957 Defence White Paper signalled the change. It was decided to concentrate on the defence of V-Bomber bases and this meant Tangmere was in the wrong place.

Fighter Command's Air Chief Marshal Sir Thomas Pike reviewed the 1958 parade. The Station C.O., Group Captain R.I.K. Edwards, was in command of an impressive march past, while Spitfires and Hurricanes flew overhead.

Among the large crowd watching were war-time ace Johnny Johnson, Mayor and Mayoress Charles and Marjorie Newell and Air Vice-Marshal T.A. Langford-Sainsbury of Selsey, who organised the Berlin Airlift.

Chichester's pride, No. 1 Squadron, which took part with No. 34 Squadron in the ill-fated 1956 Suez operation, had an association with Tangmere going back to the Twenties. One of its C.O.'s was another war-time ace, Squadron Leader Dizzy Allen.

No. 43 Squadron, which fought in both World Wars, spent 25 years at Tangmere until moved to Leuchers, Scotland, in November 1950. Its badge incorporating a fighting cock, it became known as the Fighting Cocks, jokingly referred to by No. 1 Squadron men as the 'Sussex Chicken Farmers.'

For so long part of Chichester, the Station was fittingly presented with the Freedom of the City in May 1960. Its inglorious end came when the Property Services Agency auctioned it off in 1979.

SGT. PILOT CRIPPEN, a not very friendly bull terrier, decorated with the DFM, was Tangmere's mascot and woe betide any airman who tried to move him from his chair in the Sergeant's Mess. Newcomers were challenged to try, on the promise of a drink. They found the warrant officer less fearsome.

south street
church bulldozed

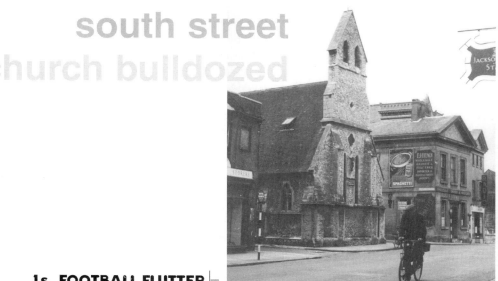

1s. FOOTBALL FLUTTER

The century old St. Richard's R.C. Church, South Street, was demolished in July 1959 to be replaced by the Cawley Road building, for which parishioners helped pay by a 1s.-a-go football flutter. The site became Colbourne's TV and radio shop (later Rumbelows and Escom).

F.J. French's wholesale grocers and fruiterers on the opposite corner was used by Mason's Garage as a showroom (lately Soupson).

Church helper **Mrs. Eileen Slade** was sorry to see the demolition, wishing the Church could have been used, perhaps, for a parish room. "But there was a need to cater for growing numbers. Good Friday congregations used to spill on to the pavement and wedding groups had to pose in the street for photographs."

Parish Priest in the Fifties, Father Pieter Tak, a Dutchman, short of stature, did not regard the lottery as gambling because it was not depriving families of necessities. It was immediately popular when it was started in 1957 and by the following year 6,000 were taking part.

Thousands of pounds were raised so that Father Langton Fox was able to announce in October 1959 that the Parish was free from debt.

Builders had finished the shell and essential furnishings of the Church and Presbytery. Over half the £50,000 had come from the lottery. Projects costing another £45,000 went ahead.

Towards the end of the decade progress was being made with a £26,000 primary school and pupils were gradually transferring from the small St. Paul's Road classrooms, which became a Catholic Club.

Most of the money for the old Church came from the savings of the pious and industrious Anne Henshall and Mary Parsons. During demolition the remains of the first parish priest, Father Wilkinson, and the Countess of Newburgh (94), who bought the land, were found in lead coffins under the sanctuary.

CHURCH SiTE SOLD FOR £3,000

Dis-used St. Peter the Less (now Hoopers), one of five 'little churches', was regrettably bulldozed in 1957.

The North Street site had been auctioned the previous year for what now seems the paltry sum of £3,000. With the incorporation of St. Peter's House nextdoor and a vegetable plot at the back, a new road called, St. Peters, was cut through from Priory Road.

Another 'little church', St. Martin's, was destroyed in 1904 and the site turned into a small walled garden (still there). Uses were found for the other three. St. Olave's, the oldest building in Chichester (1050) became a Christian bookshop in 1958. Thirteenth century All Saints, the only Chichester church to be mentioned in the Domesday Book, was turned into a Red Cross centre at a cost of £6,000-£7,000. St. Andrew's, damaged by a bomb in 1943, is now a handsome arts centre.

BRiGADE'S 999 AMBULANCE SERViCE

Operating from make-shift premises with only four ambulances, Chichester St. John Ambulance men and women ran a first-class emergency service for casualties right through the Fifties. Even though they had no radio control they were quickly at a scene. They were sad when, in 1963, County Hall made it an official, full-time, salaried service.

Feeling against the change was strong, but it was inevitable because of population rises and traffic growth. The number of calls was rising from a few a day to several hundred a week. There was concern that weekend and evening cover for the large area, including coastal villages, was dependant on volunteers.

Oscar Lake, who spent nearly half a century with ambulances and was cadet superintendent, remembered the inadequacies of the old headquarters in Combes' yard in the Hornet. The staff had just three rooms and there was garaging for only three ambulances and a lean-to for two more.

After hours calls were taken by Supt. Herbie Bridle at his South Street newsagents. Yet, despite the fact that the person on duty had to get from home to the Hornet HQ and wait for a colleague, an ambulance was on the road in four minutes.

AMBULANCES ABLE, BAKER, CHARLIE, DOG

Cadets gained experience by going out with ambulance crews at the age of 14. They could become seniors at 16.

Containing 250-300 men and women and boy and girl cadets, Chichester Division was the largest in West Sussex. It was very happy, inspections and examinations being intermingled with social functions. Senior and junior football teams added to the spirit of comradeship.

Raymond (Tubby) Clayton, who started as a cadet and became superintendent, got the Charity Commissioners to agree to the sale of a house left by Divisional Surgeon Dr. Harley Gough to enable Barford House to be provided as a new headquarters.

ABOVE: *THE BRIGADE FILLED EAST STREET FOR THE 1950 COUNTY CRICKET AND CARNIVAL WEEK PROCESSION. NOTE THE CADET BAND.*

LEFT: *NURSING CADETS DRILL CUP SUCCESS 1955*

BOBBiES ON THE BEAT

CHICHESTER'S BEST KNOWN BOBBIE

CITY POLICE 'C' SECTION 1957

SID REYNOLDS

Far from being armed, policemen in the Fifties were father figures, Dixons of Dock Green. They patrolled the town on foot, helped old ladies and children across the road, gave advice and dealt with petty offenders in their own way on the spot.

Archie Tilling, who spent much of his life as a sergeant in the Army or the Police, recalled the happy days of the real Bobby-on-the Beat: "There was a great relationship between police and public and between the police themselves, so it was a happy job.

"We didn't have to be afraid of being charged with assault if we needed to check somebody severely. Not that we were brutal. We were firm but compassionate. I did not have any trouble during the Teddy Boy era. If somebody was awkward we took them home by the ear for their parents to punish."

In Chichester there were 20-30 uniformed men, four CID officers and a small traffic section with the veteran Sgt. Felix Morris in charge of a few Rileys and motorcycles. Single speed sit-up-and-beg Raleigh bikes were issued.

In the absence of radio, phone boxes were used to maintain links, but it was still possible to get a policeman within 15 minutes. Anyway, crime levels were lower and officers had better control, keeping an eye on known criminals. Sentences were severe enough to be a strong deterrent.

Pay was under £10 a week, but there were allowances for boots (3s. a week) and plain clothes. Army style pay parades were held, the men having to salute, answer questions on efficiency and undergo a long session of parade ground drill.

Pamela Baker, one of only two West Sussex policewomen, was a familiar figure on her cycle, until, in 1952 she got her own car. "My pay was £3.10s. a week, plus £1 for lodging. During my service I was punched and kicked and attacked with a chopper and scissors. When I responded to a call that a naked man was wandering along the A27 I wrapped a blanket round him and took him to Graylingwell Hospital."

POLICE HQ UPSTAIRS

Before the Sussex police forces were amalgamated into a single control at Lewes, West Sussex Constablury HQ was in a few rooms upstairs in Chichester Police Station. There were 500 officers in West Sussex when the Constablury reached its centenary in March 1957. They were catching 4,000 criminals a year. Chief Constable R. Paterson Wilson had only a small headquarters staff. An Indian Police officer, he looked a colonial type with a moustache, but, though autocratic and efficient, he was kind and stopped to speak to his men. He, personally, appointed everybody.

Living quarters were provided at the Police Station, for a superintendent in the right hand wing and for an inspector in the left hand wing. The club room was in the Police Station until the Ranch House was built in the early Sixties.

Sport was encouraged. Big burly policemen formed a successful tug-o-war team and there were football and cricket elevens. Police balls and sports days were strong annual features.

FOUR DETECTIVES IN *1954 WITH THEIR BRAND NEW AUSTIN SOMERSET*

39

Before moving into the £40,000 Northgate Fire Station in 1966 firefighters had to put up with a leaky corrugated iron cattle shed by the market. But, although it was the worst looking fire station in the West Sussex Brigade, it was most efficient. Chichester came first in all sections of the 1959 Brigade efficiency competitions.

"When it rained the place leaked," recalled **Leading Firewoman Binny Wilson**, who had put in 16 years service when she left in 1957. "The walls were lined with matchboarding. We had to cross Market Road to an old Nissan hut for the messroom and recreation and washing facilities. But there were great feelings of comradeship and no-one ever complained. We organised childrens' parties for Christmas and played volleyball."

There were 16 whole-timers in red and blue watches, working 24 hour shifts for what today seems just a few pounds a week. They and the dozen or so part-timers were under Station Officer Owen Cole (subsequently Bill Talmage), who insisted on high standards of drill and training and ensured the seven appliances and all the hoses and other equipment were A1.

JULY 1953

City firemen pose with their medals at a long service awards ceremony in July 1953.
Left to right:
Standing - Len Wilson, Bert Budd, Ted Gardner, Fred Crees, Don Roman, Tally Hill.
Seated - Cecil Doick, John New, Owen Cole, Arthur Ede, Ivor Snell.

The buildings had to be serviceable, clean and tidy and decorated as well as possible. They had been cattle sheds and market selling quarters until 1923 when the fire station was moved from East Street.

While parts were centrally heated, it was cold in the back appliance room where the AFS and spare equipment was kept.

Engineers trying to service fire engines from West Sussex stations had little room to manoeuvre. They moved to Rowe's old garage in the Hornet (now Kwik-Fit), which the County Council bought for workshops in 1957, for £15,000.

FiFTiES FiRES

Royal Sussex Regimental silver was saved but an historic Regimental picture was lost in a fire caused by an electrical fault in Chichester Barracks' Officers' Mess in December 1951. The lounge was destroyed and the other quarters were rendered unusable.

Thanks to prompt action by neighbours with a ladder, the Terry family and their pet Collie were rescued from their blazing Northgate barbers shop in January 1953. A cigarette end set a sofa alight.

Spilled lighter fuel ignited by an electric fire exploded in a sheet of flame, causing a fierce blaze at Marsh's tobacconists, East Street, in January 1953. The building was badly damaged and over £1,000 worth of stock was destroyed.

CiTY GAS WAS FiRST

Coke was a cheap by-product from the very efficient Stockbridge Road gas works (now earmarked for homes). **Alec Stalker**, who worked there as a stoker, remembered people paying a few pence for a pram load to burn on their fires.

Four retort burners, 10ft. tall, were fed with coal to make crude gas, which was stored ready for use in two large gas holders just below the railway line.

Mr. Stalker: "We worked in shifts shovelling coal from railway wagons at the station and unloading it at the gas works for burning. It was a dirty job, causing blisters on your hands, and, although a bath was provided, the smell of gas lingered.

"We had to keep shovelling the coal into the burners and de-clinkering them. You could tell when people were cooking Sunday dinners by the falling level of the gas holders."

Chichester Gas Company was a pioneer in the production of gas and, thanks to its efficiency, and up-to-date equipment, it lit up the City a week before Portsmouth.

The gas price went up by 1d. a therm in August 1957 - equal to 4d. a week for the average housewife

300-YEAR-OLD GROCERS

To shop at Sharp Garland, Eastgate Square, was to step into a past age, generations before supermarkets. Of derelict appearance, it certainly looked the oldest grocers in the country with supplies in hessian sacks and the all-pervading smell of roasting coffee.

The shop was nearing its end in the Fifties and, now, the only reminder of times past is the name, 'Sharp Garland House' given to a block of flats behind 'The Bazaar'.

Four generations of Garlands had owned the shop. Sir Archibald Garland was Mayor seven times and his father, Mr. Sharp Garland, five times The last of the family, Miss Cora Garland, died of cancer in 1957 and, although the manager, Alfred Peat (72), an antiquarian, who started there as a 5s. a week apprentice, took it over in a surprise development, closure came early the next decade. It was pulled down as unsafe in 1964, just one year short of its 300th anniversary.

Hairdresser Michael Kent, whose parents were friends of Miss Garland, recalled, "I went to the shop as a young lad with my mother. The smell of coffee wafted along East Street. Tea, sugar and other goods were kept in large tins at the back. In front of the two counters were rows of biscuit tins. Several brands of tea were available because people drank mostly tea."

HiGH CLASS AT CHi-HiGH

If there had been performance league tables in the Fifties the 700-strong Chichester Boys' High School would have been well to the top. Its inclusion in The Times Educational Supplement list of Oxbridge Open Award winners along with well known independent schools indicated academic excellence.

Headmaster for 20 years, the very efficient Kenneth Anderson (KD), believed in examinations, feeling they were a healthy stimulus to intellectual achievement.

He reported at the 1955 speech day that 25 of 32 leavers had gone to university and four state scholarships and 16 county scholarships had been awarded.

"We had an excellent record, but then we had an exceptionally good staff," Mr. Anderson recalled. "At the same time, we did not neglect the less able, many of whom took responsible positions at the top of the school and went to university. The school gained an impressive list of awards and scholarships and it was a pleasure to be headmaster there."

Of smart military bearing, sporting a moustache, KD was a war-time Royal Signals Major. He maintained strict discipline, severely punishing wrongdoers, and insisting on proper school uniform and prompt timekeeping. During the decade the Parents' Association was formed.

When comprehensive schooling came in 1971 he was appointed Head of the combined High School and Lancastrian School.

Head of Science Geoffrey Marwood remembered Mr. Anderson as a very efficient headmaster who certainly achieved results. Erect and of great personal dignity, he walked well and expected others to follow his examples.

French Teacher and Sports Coach Frank Haill: "I came to Chichester when the Henry Thornton School was evacuated from Clapham and, finding it a fine school, I spent the remaining 27 years of my career there".

GiRLS' SCHOOL NUMBERS DOUBLE

Golden Jubilee celebrations, resulting in the provision of a fine swimming pool, were the culmination of a memorable decade for Chichester Girls' High School. Numbers grew from a war-time 400, to 700 in 1950, and nearly 800 in 1956, making the building burst at the seams. In fact, with no room large enough, it was never possible for the whole school to meet together.

Temporary classrooms had to be built and the Gaumont Cinema was hired for speech days. Miss Enid Dynes, a London science graduate, arrived as Headmistress in 1953 from a Birmingham girls' grammar school.

MISS DYNES

Deputy Headmistress Miss Monica Lee remembered the way Miss Dynes never spared herself for the school. Kind, generous and an excellent organiser, she achieved a great deal and ensured excellent academic results. One innovation was the formation of a 6th Form Society with the Boys' High School. A joint committee was set up and meetings were held in each school.

Golden Jubilee celebrations in 1959 included a school picnic, an evening dinner and a Cathedral thanksgiving service. The financial object, £1,500 for a swimming pool, was achieved, so the pool opened in 1961.

When Miss Dynes retired in 1971 Miss Pamela King was appointed Headmistress. Miss Dynes died in 1991 aged 82.

Gym Slip Tarzans.

Girls climbing trees is hardly an activity you would expect to see at a girls' grammar school, but Miss Ruth Matson (Matty), the innovative predecessor to Miss Dynes, saw it as good physical exercise.

English teacher Mrs. Peggy Richardson recalled that, while other heads would have been afraid of falls, the much loved Matty believed the girls would be safe as long as they did not panic. "She wanted a caretaker who could talk them down safely and, thanks to Mr. Cotton, none ever fell. She was an imaginative, courageous and excellent head without pride or side. Her open-minded and broad outlook brought a wind of change to the school.

"The girls liked Matty and she did not need to be unnecessarily hard with them because what she did they approved of. To her each pupil was a person in her own right. She was so different from any head I have known."

Tall and large, Miss Matson presented a somewhat masculine appearance in tweedy clothes, happily riding an old fashioned motorcycle to and from home in Summersdale and also into the country. She was always ready to try something new and her free choice afternoons, when pupils picked their own subjects, was an advance for those times. She died on New Years Day 1967 aged 71.

TWO NEW SCHOOLS AT KiNGSHAM

When the Lancastrian Boys' and Girls' Schools were in brand new buildings on former Kingsham farmland during the decade the City boasted the best in secondary modern schooling facilities.

Traditions of excellence initiated by pioneering educationalist Joseph Lancaster in the 1880s were carried forward in well equipped classrooms surrounded by large playing fields. Good academic, sporting and social achievements were a credit to the staffs.

Comprehensive education was then over a decade away (1971). Those who look back with pleasure at the two Lancastrian Schools' history wish that at least the name, Lancastrian, could somehow have been incorporated in the titles of the comprehensive schools.

Boys' School too small

Rising pupil numbers meant that the £135,000 Boys' School, which opened in 1955, was not big enough.

By 1959 the roll had doubled to 600 and so many children were still entering secondary education that classes had to be formed back in the hard pressed Orchard Street premises (now Chichester Central CE School).

Head of Lower School, Len Stubbs, recalled, "Calculations were out due mainly to the substantial number of Service families at Tangmere and other bases. We had to resort to Orchard Street for four years. Some 200 Lancastrian boys were there. Then Bishop Luffa School pupils moved in while their school was being built."

lancastrian boys school staff

[headmaster : Roy Lewis]

Boys achieved rising academic standards in the new school. An O-Level course was started and in the Sixties pupils were even taking A-levels.

"It was a very good school with a marvellous spirit," recalled **History Teacher Eric Ponting,** who was there for 38 years, retiring in 1974.

Headmaster Roy Lewis, a radio ham, pioneered the idea of secondary modern pupils taking public examinations. His appointment had been a surprise because he had not graduated and, having come from a primary school in Wisborough Green, was not experienced with pupils over 11. However, he achieved good results.

Deputy Headmaster was Don Hanson, who had many years experience and was prominent in the Scout movement. The amalgamation with the High School to form, the comprehensive school resulted in a roll of 1,400. Mr. Lewis retired.

'Honour Before Honours'

The progressive Miss Beatrice Tattersill, who succeeded the war-time Headmistress, Miss E. Trott, in 1949, took the Lancastrian Girls to Kingsham in 1958. She broadened the curriculum, introducing GCE and, later, CSE examinations, and transferring a dozen or so more advanced girls every year to the High School 6th Form.

Proud of the School, Miss Tattersill expected high standards of work and behaviour in accordance with the great Lancastrian tradition.

In contrast to the Nineties' mini-skirts, the navy blue uniforms had to be of modest length and hair-styles sensible.

English Teacher Mrs. Betty Broadbridge, who later became the Comprehensive School Deputy Headmistress, found it a very happy school with vitality and good humour. 'Honour Before Honours' was an appropriate motto. Mrs. Marjorie Fuller, who had been deputy to Miss Tattersill, was very creative and wrote a school hymn. The two had the same good standards and worked in close harmony.

Miss Pamela King became the first Headmistress of the 1,400 strong girls' comprehensive, but had to take early retirement for health reasons in 1980. Then she entered the Church and, at St. Peter and St. Paul, was one of the first women parish deacons in the country. She died in 1993. Miss Tattersill died in April 1996.

DR. BiSHOP BECAME A ViCAR

Changing career in his sixties, Dr. Edgar Bishop left the headmaster's study to enter the pulpit. He was only the second headmaster of Chichester Boys' High School and when he retired at 61 in 1953 he had been there 19 years. From 350 pupils and a staff of 18 the School doubled in size.

Noted for his insistence on promptness, Dr. Bishop stood, watch in hand, timing staff arrivals and class movements. A city magistrate, he was appointed chairman of the Juvenile Court.

After his ordination by Bishop Bell in the Cathedral in 1956, he was appointed Curate of St. Paul's. The following year he became Vicar of Oving, Tangmere and Merston.

CHARLIE MEETS THE QUEEN

A never-to-be-forgotten moment for man-of-the-people **Charlie Newell** as the Queen shakes hands in Priory Park during the 1956 Royal visit. He was introduced by Mayor Leslie Evershed-Martin, Festival Theatre founder, whom he succeeded as Mayor in 1957.

Charlie was often in the limelight, speaking his mind in easily understood terms. He never spared himself during his long council service or many voluntary efforts for the community. Recognition came with the presentation of the City Freedom at the age of 50 in 1971.

The ex-RAF man and insurance agent described the Fifties when he and wife Marjorie were busily shaping events, as an exciting, marvellous decade. During their two years as Chief Citizens they carried out an average of one engagement a day.

Pensioners are grateful to him for forming a Pensioners' Association and helping to provide a rest room in the Hornet. Later, thanks to Council colleague Edgar Tozer and a good response to an appeal, £20,000 was raised for the Newell Centre, which opened in 1968.

The former White Rose Concert Party entertainer was appointed a JP and served for 27 years, becoming Chairman of the Licensing Magistrates. Sport was another of his interests and he was President of the Gilbertian Cricket Club and Chairman of both Chichester City FC and Chichester FC Supporters' Club.

HUNDREDS DANCED iN THE NEW YEAR

Happy memories of Chichester's thriving community life in the Fifties, recalled by the 1952 Mayoress, **Mrs. Eileen Worley,** include social, charity and sporting occasions, dinners and dances and many evening events staged by the host of voluntary organisations.

The House of Kimbell, Dolphin and Anchor Hotel and Unicorn were busy centres of activity. On New Year's Eve 1952 Mrs. Worley and her late husband, Frank, were guests at three dances. Seven hundred were at Graylingwell Hospital and 200 at St. Richard's Hospital nurses dance at County Hall.

Another big crowd of revellers raised a lot of money for charity at the Round Table dance.

"Although it was hard work, we had a wonderful year, full of interest," Mrs. Worley recalled.

Community strength was shown by the generous response to Mayor Worley's flood disaster appeals for East Anglia and Lynton and Lynmouth. Moved by the loss of life and property, people gave van loads of clothing, bedding and other necessities for luckless victims.

Collections were made at cinemas and football grounds, firemen toured the streets collecting and the Mayoress organised a house-to-house collection. Altogether, the City raised £1,500 for the East coast disaster fund and nearly £700 for Lynton and Lynmouth.

Mr. Worley was doubly honoured that year - elected alderman as well as mayor. Watching the Council ceremony were the couple's two children, Ian (8) and Ann (4). A chartered accountant, he was Chairman of Chichester and District Angling Society and a Rotarian. He died in 1966 aged 59.

DANCiNG AT COUNTY HALL

Workers tripped the light fantastic at County Hall on Tuesday evenings. Their duties over for the day, they would take to the fine floor of the Council Chamber and dance.

A committee with Marjorie Maidment as secretary ran sequence dancing for West Sussex Guild of Officers (NALGO). The first dance leaders were Jack and Hilda Johnson. They were succeeded by Ray and Barbara Gambling and then Jim and Elsie Brookes, who ran other dances in the area.

It was a wonderful venue for dancing and 50-60 took part. Twice a year there was a ball and everybody dressed in evening wear. The end came when the floor was carpeted as part of alterations.

TORY REBELS BACKED DOWN

Rebels well and truly rocked the Tory boat in the Fifties. There was even talk of a right winger fighting the 'out-of-touch' MP, Lancelot Joynson-Hicks, for the ultra safe Chichester seat in 1958.

Although comments went on for sometime, they eventually petered out and Flansham farmer Walter Loveys (37), County Councillor and Divisional Tory Chairman, was chosen as candidate.

Some thought there were better candidates, but he won the 1958 By-Election caused by Joynson-Hicks' succession to the title, Viscount Brentford, and he also won a thumping majority in the 'quiet' 1959 General Election, remaining as MP for most of the Sixties.

Criticism of Joynson-Hicks was that he lived in East Sussex and worked in his London solicitor's office, so he did not meet people in the streets to discuss their problems. Conservatives had to be democratic and appeal to the working class.

Son of the Twenties Home Secretary (Jix), Joynson-Hicks first became Chichester MP at a 1942 By-Election. He was made a Baronet in 1955, resigning his £1,500 a year appointment as Parliamentary Secretary to the Ministry of Fuel. His majorities were 16,000 in 1950, 18,000 in 1951 and 18,000 in 1955.

1958 By-Election - Loveys 23,158, Edgar Simpkins (Lab) 9,504.

1959 General Election - Loveys 30,755, John Spooner (Lab) 9,546, Jackson Newman (Lib) 6,913.

SORTiNG OFFiCE WAS CREEPY

Ghostly goings-on at the creaky old GPO Sorting Office (now G A Property Services) made the postmen nervy. They sometimes heard strange footsteps in the early hours and at a nearby tobacconist's flat a figure had been seen apparently disappearing through a wall.

Retired Postman David Linn, who started as a £1.4s.6d. a week telegram boy: "Men said it was haunted and I, myself, found it eerie. On your own at night you could hear footsteps overhead and it was not just creaking floorboards."

Over 60 men worked in the building, handling 50 bags of incoming and outgoing mail a day in difficult conditions. Thousands of letters for delivery had to be hauled up a lift shaft by pulley ready for sorting upstairs. The daily average for first delivery was 30,000 letters and 8,000 parcels.

For about £6 a week men went out putting them through letter boxes in the large area from the downs to the coast. A fleet of cycles was kept in the basement for city and local village deliveries.

Postage then cost 2d. to 3d. and everything was delivered the next day.

Most mail was transported by rail, Redhill being the centre for Sussex. This meant meeting trains at the station, starting at 3am-4am.

For Christmas, 150 casuals, mostly students, were taken on. Work started at 3am on Christmas morning and, with a Christmas Day delivery, went on most of the day.

Resident at Binderton House, near Lavant, Foreign Secretary Anthony Eden (later Lord Avon) sent a letter to telephonists and postmen in 1952 thanking them for their excellent service during his convalescence. The girls wired him their congratulations on his wedding to Clarrisa Spencer-Churchill, an event which led to him leaving Binderton.

During the Fifties there were 30-40 Hello Girls at the West Street GPO switchboards and 10 girls and half-a-dozen delivery boys operated a telegram service from 8am to 8pm. Re-armament caused a shortage of cable and other equipment, so there were 73 waiting for a phone.

CiTY OWNED DELL QUAY

Picturesque Chichester Harbour was a Corporation responsibility carried out by **Harbourmaster Freddie Hard** and the Council Harbour Committee. The Council owned the priceless assets of Dell Quay and part of Itchenor foreshore and it also had an important admin' role.

From the harbour entrance, round Thorney Island, Bosham and Fishbourne stretches, and back to the entrance, via Dell Quay and Itchenor, is a distance of 17 miles, encompassing an area of outstanding natural beauty, a haven for wildlife and a mecca for yachtsmen.

The operation fell on the rates because the Harbour Committee could not manage every year on its £3,000 budget. However, yachting was taking off in the Fifties and Sixties and, with 8,000 craft on the water, accounts were breaking even when the Harbour Conservancy was set up in 1971.

The £500 a year harbourmaster was responsible for controlling shipping, enforcing byelaws, collecting harbour dues and patrolling in his specially built 27ft. launch, on the look-out for water ski-ers breaking the six knot speed limit.

"It was a 24 hours-a-day job, especially in summer, sometimes involving life saving." recalled Lieut. Comdr. Hard, who, during 29 years in the Royal Navy was in charge of big ocean tugs. "I just had a secretary, Ann Fox, a charge hand and two men."

He took over in 1957 from Capt. R.H. Milward and served until retirement in 1978. During his five years as Harbourmaster Capt. Milward surveyed the waters to update charts, laid visitors' buoys and piloted two 2,500 floating docks bound for Holland.

GAVE CiTY iTS MUSEUM

Prominent architect, Tory rebel, tough magistrate, questioning councillor, conservationist - with many attributes, **Stanley Roth** did a lot for the City. He served on both County and City Councils and was Magistrates' Court Chairman for nine years.

His conservation ideas saved Little London, providing the City with its museum, and could have saved Somerstown, which some were condemning as slums.

Colleague Terry Roberts pointed out: "In the Fifties and Sixties conservation was not a buzz word and there is no doubt old churches and buildings, which were then pulled down, would not have bitten the dust today.

"Although Mr. Roth was decisive, forceful and definite, he was always fair and a pleasure to work with. As an architect, he was a traditionalist, not a modernist, which explains his keenness to save interesting parts of old Chichester."

Mrs. Pat Roth agreed that fairness was one of her husband's great qualities, as shown by his magisterial work, for which he was awarded the MBE. "He appeared controversial and rebellious because he would not accept things as gospel unless he knew them to be true. He could not be a yes-man, but he was certainly not quarrelsome."

Mr. Roth (86 when he died in 1993) fought to overcome the effects of injuries received from an exploding land mine during Monty's victorious 1942 push at El Alamein. Work for the community was a replacement for sporting activity.

Realising the potential of an old Little London granary for a museum, he bought it, carefully converted it and leased it to the City Council for 21 years at £1,300 a year.

He loved Little London and wanted to save it. When the Council condemned half-a-dozen cottages at the end of the street he bought them for £100 each and restored them, making them worth a lot of money.

The destruction of 119 houses, shops and pubs at Somerstown for redevelopment upset him because they could have been turned into very desirable homes. In fact, he produced a plan showing Cross Street with a square and trees.

GUNS AND SPORTS SHOP

Well known in Chichester in the Fifties, Russell Hillsdon, South Street, was the Sports Store of the South. Selling guns and cartridges, the business was established in 1920 in Barnham Cattle Market. In 1922 a shop was opened at 30 South Street (now Oddbins), where all sports equipment was sold, although the heart of the firm was the gun department.

Under Mr. Hillsdon's management the business survived the war and 1946 saw the start of a new era.

Immediately opposite No. 30, the old Cafe Royal was purchased and, despite post-war planning restrictions, a fine new shop (now Lakeland Plastics) was opened before large crowds in 1950.

All departments were expanded. The ground floor was devoted entirely to sports equipment, including tennis rackets (some strung on the premises), cricket bats by the hundred, football, hockey, squash, lacrosse and darts.

In October and November vast quantities of fireworks were sold over the counter and large displays went to clubs and schools over a wide area. No smoking and other safety measures were applied and a watch was kept for under-age purchasers.

At Christmas a limited range of toys, including Hornby trains, Meccano and Scalextric were featured and games like Monopoly and Scrabble were in good demand.

A wide staircase led to the gun department where a great selection of shotguns, rifles, air rifles and accessories, plus clothing, was available, with a 'try gun' for measuring customers' special requirements. The demand for cartridges increased and sales well exceeded the million a year mark.

Repairs were carried out on the premises in a well equipped workshop staffed by skilled gunsmiths. Fishing rods and tackle were stocked and live bait, imported at weekends, attracted many customers.

For ladies, also on the first floor, there was swim wear and tennis wear and a vast range of clothing from well known agencies, including Aquascutum and Daks. Offices and stores occupied the second floor.

The business closed in 1984 when Mr. Hillsdon retired after 64 years, during which he had seen many changes. Cartridge prices had increased from 12s.6d. per 100 to £17.50 and a best London gun from about £500 to over £15,000.

TAXMAN TOOK SADLER FORTUNES

Sadlers Walk, Chichester's first shopping arcade, was created from the first in-town garden shop, Sadlers, opened by gardening expert Percy Thrower in 1954. Corn, seed and feed merchant Fred Sadler, who started life with a horse and cart provided by his father, moved to the new shop from premises he had occupied since 1886 (now Thomas Cook).

He was a hard headed businessman, owning a lot of valuable property, but he did not safeguard his wealth and when he died, aged 95, the taxman took a lot in death duties.

His grandson, **David Sadler**, recalled: "Sadlers was a very prosperous business dealing in animal feed, corn and seeds. A feed factory at Westhampnett produced 400 tons a week for farmers in Sussex, Hampshire and Surrey.

"The business also owned factories on the Industrial Estate and at Fishbourne and a corn merchants at East Grinstead. A Little London property, now the City Museum, was a store and plant for processing farmers' grain. Henty and Constable Brewery was a big customer for a special malting barley used for the very strong 5 X brew.

"But, although grandfather was hard working and as tough as nails in business, he did not manage his affairs well and only one set of accounts a year was produced. So when he died in 1961 thousands of pounds went in death duties. The same thing happened on the death of one of his two sons, Robert, 10 years later.

"The business had to be broken up. My uncle and I tried running the garden shop for half-a-dozen years, but we could not show a profit and in 1978 it was turned into a shopping arcade."

A handsome period house, formerly offices of Town Clerk and Coroner J.W. Loader Cooper, once stood there.

A jovial character, 6ft.2ins. tall, Fred Sadler liked whisky and cricket, counting Don Bradman among his friends. Owning two Rolls Royce cars, he was driven around by chauffeur Harry Ford.

As well as the East Street shop and factories, he owned the Corn Exchange, East Pallant House, St. Martin's garden land, houses in Little London and, at one time, the Royal Norfolk Hotel, Bognor Regis.

The St. Martin's Land, where he cultivated asparagus beds and vegetables, was taken from him by compulsory purchase for £900 for car parking. East Pallant House was also compulsorily purchased for £10,000.

OBSERVER (2D.) CHANGES HANDS

Chichester Observer, published on Saturdays (later Fridays), cost 2d. through-out the decade. Those who did not like change were sorry to see Acfords sell the paper to Portsmouth and Sunderland Newspapers on April 1 1950.

Although the offices remained in the antiquated Little London building, control and printing went to Portsmouth and it was six years before Sub-Editor Jim Neal was appointed Editor. The author arrived as £10 a week Chief Reporter at the time of the change to find few staff.

An early recruit was Paddy Welsh, who became public relations officer to the County Council and, later, to Southern Water Authority. Graham Brooks began his 31 years reign as Editor in 1961.

Richmond (R.J.) Acford, a dapper little man with twinkling blue eyes, had been proprietor with Talbot Vezey Strong as Managing Director. They were sadly lacking resources and it was no surprise when they sold. Miss Marjorie Acford (daughter) was Editor and Director with the distinction of being the only woman editing a local paper during the war. Basil Acford (son) was in charge of Bognor Regis Observer.

Richmond Acford, who died in 1951 aged 82, took over the Bognor paper in 1900 and acquired Chichester Observer shortly afterwards and the Midhurst paper before World War 1. For many years he edited all three papers and also served on Chichester and Bognor Regis Councils.

Four papers circulating in Chichester in the Fifties have been lost - Chichester Post, Sussex Daily News, Southern Weekly News and Hampshire Telegraph

ELEGANT TOWN CLERK

Cutting a tall and distinguished figure, Town Clerk Eric Banks was a conscientious servant of the City for over 30 years, keen to preserve its unique identity. Chichester to him was utterly charming and historic and he was always out to do his best for it, maintaining the highest standards of civic life.

Over contentious planning issues he would even be ready to do battle with County Hall. Such was his enthusiasm for the City, he sometimes regarded the County Council as enemy. He could be very outspoken.

Geoffrey Heather: "Chichester was lucky to have had a man of his dedication and experience, noted for his own special style of sartorial elegance."

Mr. Banks was a keen churchman, a member of the Church Assembly, and he did not mind being known as a tea-totaller. Always with a ready smile and most courteous, he never got rattled and lost his temper. His was the pacifying, professional voice of reason during the crossfire of heated debate.

He was the 1956 Chairman of the Home Counties Branch of the Society of Town Clerks and in April 1957 the City Council officially congratulated him when he celebrated the 21 years of his appointment from Eastbourne.

£300,000 WATERWORKS SALE

Consumers' complaints about today's water industry could not have been applied to Chichester's efficient little waterworks department in the Fifties. Supplies were copious, the water rate did not go up for a dozen years, leakages were reduced and there were no fat cats - water engineer Alfred Burgess got £700 a year.

But change came. Government pressure for small undertakings to merge for greater efficiency resulted in the Council selling its undertaking to Portsmouth Water Company (PWC) for £300,000.

That included, mainly, Fishbourne pumping station, the £48,500 Funtington pumping station and reservoirs.

Mr. Burgess and his staff of 20 were taken on by PWC, but the Tower Street distribution depot was closed.

In 1951 the two pumping stations' capacity was over 3m. gallons a day, well in excess of average demand.

Nearly 80 square miles were served, north to the downs and south to the coast. In addition, water was sold by meter to a small Selsey company with a water tower. Such was the efficiency of the operation and leakage detection that 10 years after Mr. Burgess's appointment in 1945 water consumption had not gone up.

Now 91 and living at Teignmouth he recalled: "I was able to keep close tabs on everything. We had four uniformed inspectors who went round on cycles checking for leaks and ensuring bye-laws were being complied with. If workmen got 1p. an hour increase in their £6-£8 a week wages that was something."

CANAL SOLD FOR £7,500

The 4-mile long, spring fed Chichester Canal was sold by the City Council to the County Council in 1957 for £7,500. City councillors were not sorry to part with it because it was costing £600 a year maintenance and practically all of it lay in the Rural Council area.

The County needed to buy because Donnington and Birdham road bridges had to be safeguarded against navigation rights and also because there was talk of road improvements at the Basin.

In 1956 London Anglers' Association was interested in buying, but did not proceed because of the onerous maintenance problem, which had earlier caused Chichester anglers to withdraw.

Canal Society Treasurer Mrs. Linda Wilkinson was glad the waterway went to the County Council because that later gave the Society the opportunity to lease it for a peppercorn rent in 1984 for recreational purposes.

The Canal was originally constructed to transport arms and was later used for coal which benefited the gas works, but the railway proved quicker and traffic stopped in 1906. The City Council finally abandoned it in 1928.

£7,200 ELECTRiCiTY PAY-OFF

Chichester received a warming £7,200 compensation for its electricity supply department under the Government's £5m. nationalisation deal. But it shivered as a result of power cuts and coal shortages.

Current was off for long periods, sometimes hours, and the half-a-dozen coal merchants struggled to eke out dwindling supplies.

The Council ran its own electricity department, with Harold Taunt as manager, from 43 North Street (now M. & W. Mack Ltd.). Southern Electricity established offices and showrooms there, advertising, *'Electricity is readily available in Chichester and District.'*

In fact, it was often off during a 1950 autumnal cold snap, frustrating office workers and householders. One load shedding caused a 4-hour interruption to Little London and Parklands areas as housewives were cooking. Even the electricity offices were hit.

Lists were published showing when particular areas would be cut off. Mr. Taunt regretted the difficulties would continue until there was enough generating plant to meet the country's needs.

Coal merchants based deliveries on house size, fixing an individual limit of 5cwts. They asked panicking householders not to grumble at them because the problems were a shortage of railway wagons and the London gas strike. D. Pennicott received only 10 tons for his large business, compared with a normal 50-60 tons a week.

THE EASTLANDS' STORY

Husband and wife Jesse and Alice Eastland, who kept the Wheatsheaf, Oving Road, put in thousands of unpaid hours for the community with their long membership of the City Council from the Twenties through the Fifties. They were each separately elected mayor.

Although firm Socialists, they stood as Independents, working for the good of all and never letting their political feelings become apparent. Recognition of their efforts came when they were made Honorary Freemen and a public dinner was held in their honour in November 1958.

Mr. Eastland was badly injured while working as a railway shunter and courageously overcame considerable disabilities. A long serving magistrate, he received the MBE for his Employment Committee work.

His wife, the City's first ever woman Mayor, was, appropriately, chief citizen for 1953 Coronation year. To mark her considerable work on the Housing Committee a Whyke Estate Road was named after her.

CANON'S BROADSIDE

St. Peter's Arcade, opposite the Cathedral, was created from the Sub-Deanery Church, where the great character, City Councillor Canon Godfrey Wells, was Vicar.

A familiar figure on his tricycle, he spoke bluntly from strong and genuinely held beliefs. Lashing out at the £2,800 spent on the 1951 Festival of Britain celebrations, he said that money could have been better used for housing.

Large congregations were attracted by his unconventional approach. Servicemen particularly liked him because, sensible and direct, he spoke their language.

Badly wounded while fighting with the Canadians during the World War 1 Battle of Vimy Ridge, he made light of considerable disabilities. Bravely, he got back in uniform for World War 2 as a Home Guardsman and Forces' Chaplain. He died in 1955 aged 64.

LiGHTS NOT ON !

A 1955 idea for putting lights at the Cross to ease growing traffic problems was given a **RED**. When police experimented to see whether it would be better if the four streets were given a **GREEN** alternately two questions became obvious - Would lights and signs spoil the scene? How would pedestrians cope?

Everyone concluded the only real answer was to get on with the ring road so drivers would not need to go through the city centre.

Pinnacles and angel and cherub heads on the Cross were crumbling so badly experts reckoned five years skilled work costing thousands was necessary. It was decided to add 1d. a year to the rates specially for repairs and to make a start by spending £800 for a stonemason to set in new Clipsham stone.

ARTS CENTRE PLAN FOUNDERED

Proudly proclaimed 'City of Culture' in the Nineties, Chichester lost an opportunity in the Fifties of having Britain's first provincial arts centre.

Plans by wealthy philanthropist George Booth, of Funtington, to turn the Baffins Lane Corn Exchange into a hall and gallery fell apart and when artist and designer **David Goodman** tried to save the day by setting up a consortium only a third of the required £1,000 capital was received in three months.

All that happened on the ground was the conversion of a barn into the Booth Rooms (now John Wiley and Sons Publishers) for Marian Lombard's dancing school.

"An enormous opportunity was lost," recalled Mr. Goodman, who was going to be arts director.

Chichester Arts Centre Ltd. finally bit the dust at the end of the 1951 Festival of Britain.

'DOWN TOWN' MAYOR

Garage boss Cecil (Gig) Herniman, a Forties Mayor of Chichester, is here wearing the chain of office as Mayor of St. Pancras Corporation - the ancient Wheelbarrow Club, which helps the Dears Almshouses charity.

Succeeding brewery boss Richard Henty, he was 'Down Town' Mayor for 1953,54,55 and 56.

Mr. Herniman claimed the unusual record of serving on all three local councils, City, Rural and County.

CiTY LOST iTS COURTS

Courts were axed early in the decade. Despite a mayoral plea, the Lord Chancellor abolished the City's 400-year-old right to hold its own Quarter Sessions. And City and County Magistrates' Courts were merged.

Last Recorder of the Quarter Sessions, which convened on Saturday mornings, was Cecil Havers, KC, father of Attorney General Lord Havers and grandfather of actor Nigel Havers. One of his last sentences in 1950 was to jail a labourer for a year for a razor attack on a newspaper reporter.

A key figure in the Court was Clerk of the Peace G.H. Boyce Peters. Tall and courteous, with great legal knowledge, he was also County Court Registrar.

The City's Magistrates' Court ceased to exist on December 31 1953. **Retired Deputy Clerk of the Magistrates Jack Price** remembered separate City and County Magistrates Court sitting alternate Tuesdays when he arrived in September 1950.

As a result of the merger there was a weekly sitting of the combined court on Tuesdays under the Chairmanship of Mr. Hugo Baxendale, a County Council Alderman and Hospital Committee Vice Chairman. Bill Booker, an ex-RAF man, formerly assistant at Rapers, solicitors, was Clerk.

Crime began to grow. There were 17 cases before West Sussex Quarter Sessions in September 1950 and it was announced that the salary of County Clerk of the Peace Tom Hayward, who was also County Council Clerk, would be put up to £500 a year because of increased work and responsibility.

Much of Judge F.K. Archer's work at Chichester County Court was housing possession cases concerning tied farm cottages and families squatting in Tangmere service quarters.

County Court judges' salaries went up from £2,800 to £4,000 a year.

ANSTIE'S
GOLD FLAKE
Cigarettes

ANSTIE'S GOLD FLAKE *Cigarettes*

Your Smoke AT – **1/4** FOR TEN

A.N.3A

SMOKING AND DRINKING IN THE FIFTIES

*NO HEALTH WARNINGS ON THE CIGARETTE PACKETS
AND THE PRICE DID NOT GO UP MUCH.*

*FOUNDED IN THE 1800s, PINKS WAS FAMED FOR
GINGER BEER PRODUCED AT MELBOURNE ROAD.*

*OLD WESTGATE BEFORE AVENUE DE CHARTRES CUT ACROSS WESTGATE FIELDS TO A NEW ROUNDABOUT.
CHARLIE HOOKER'S SWEET SHOP, THE OLD TOLL HOUSE (NOW INDIAN COTTAGE RESTAURANT), WAS SPARED,
BUT THE BUILDING TO THE RIGHT FELL TO THE BULLDOZER.*

Chichester in the **1950s**

EAST STREET HAD CLOSED FOR THE DAY AS THE CAMERAMAN LOOKED BACK TOWARDS THE CITY CROSS, TO SHOW - INTERNATIONAL STORES (GROCERS, MANAGER ALBERT CUTTER), LEWIS (TOBACCONIST), MASTERS AND COMPANY (OUTFITTERS), E.H. LEWIS AND SON LTD. (JEWELLERS), MACFISHERIES, LACEYS (PRINTERS AND STATIONERS), MAYPOLE (GROCERS) AND KIMBELL AND SONS (SAUSAGES). ABOVE THE INTERNATIONAL WAS THE CHURCHILL ROOM AND CONSERVATIVE OFFICES (MAJOR GERALD ACTON, CONSERVATIVE AGENT).

SHIPPAMS' 1957 OFFICE BUILDING WORK TOOK IN C. BIFFIN'S FRUIT AND FLOWER SHOP, THE SNACK BAR AND THE PROPERTY NEXT DOOR.

APPROACHING THE CROSS ALONG SOUTH STREET, PROBABLY 1954, ARE: CURRYS CYCLE AND RADIO SHOP (MANAGER MR. HENDERSON); EMILE, LADIES' AND GENTS HAIRDRESSER (ALFRED LEE); BUSHBYS, TOBACCONIST (FRANK BUSHBY); BISHOP BROTHERS (SHOES), LATER CHICHESTER OBSERVER OFFICES; AND A.E. SPURRIER AND SON, BAKERS.

EASTGATE SQUARE SHOPS IN JULY 1959 - GOODRIDGE AND CO. (WILLIAM GOODRIDGE), MOTOR CYCLE SPECIALISTS, NOW SUSSEX CAMERA CENTRE; A CAFE WHICH HAD BEEN THE YORKSHIRE PANTRY; GEORGE BEVIS, PHOTOGRAPHIC CHEMIST; NORMAN FOX, TAILOR; AND G. PINE, IRONMONGER.

LENNARDS SHOE SHOP (NOW GOLD ARTS, JEWELLERS, LTD.) ON A CITY CROSS CORNER, WAS PROPPED UP WITH HEAVY TIMBERS BECAUSE IT LOOKED DANGEROUS AT THE END OF THE DECADE, BUILDERS WERE UNABLE TO SAVE IT, SO THE COUNCIL HAD NO ALTERNATIVE BUT TO AGREE TO DEMOLITION AND RE-BUILDING.

BOYS' CLUB THRiVED - GiRLS' CLUB FAiLED

While Chichester Boys' Club grew, the Girls' Club had problems, particularly over a meeting place and the effects of TV.

Its fine new building in Little London and record membership made the Boys' Club the best in Sussex and one of the best in the country. But the Girls' Club leader, Miss R.B. Shaw, reported in 1956 that membership was down and treasurer Guy Reynolds was sad that no new responsibilities could be taken on without more public support.

Leader of the Boys' Club since 1928, Bassil Shippam, boss of Shippams, was awarded the MBE in 1957 for dedicated service to the Boys' Club at city, county and national level.

Denis Burgess, who succeeded him in 1966, remembered, "His heart was in the Club and he worked very hard for it. A kind, delightful man, always ready to listen to peoples' problems, he was held in high regard throughout the movement."

Membership in 1955 reached a record 150 and there were fine successes by the football and cricket teams.

Highlight of that year was the opening of an £8,000 extension - a memorial to the 44 old boys killed during World War 2. Record runner Chris Chataway, chairman of the Boys' Clubs' National Federation, who became Chichester MP, performed the opening ceremony.

TWO SAiLORS MEET

The Queen listens as the Duke of Edinburgh chats to City Councillor Bill Brookes during the 1956 Royal visit to Chichester.

Mr.Brookes was Yeoman of Signals, Royal Navy, and, serving with the Grand Fleet, saw the German surrender of 1918. During the more peaceful Fifties, while a Post Office inspector, he helped form Apuldram Fishing and Boating Club and became its secretary.

One of a family of 16, he was founder of St. Pancras Community Association and a hard worker for the Twinning, Gala and Legion. In recognition of his 16 years council service and their joint community work he and his wife, Mabel, were chosen as Mayor and Mayoress in 1963 and 64.

LiLLYWHiTES LOST THEiR HOME

Happy days when Chichester City FC played in Priory Park before a thousand or two spectators came to an unfortunate end. The Lillywhites used to run out to, 'The March of the Gladiators,' from an old record player to face top teams in the good standard Sussex County League.

Spectators paid 'a bob' to watch and takings were enough to keep the club going.

But ambitious desires for semi-professional football led to the formation in 1953 of rival Chichester United and a bitter clash developed over the Saturday use of the Park.

The result was that both teams had to move to Oaklands Park and support there was never the same.

When United folded, unable to find the £5 a week expenses for their pitch, the effort seemed regrettably pointless. City remained assuredly amateur.

"United forced the issue and the sad outcome was no-one could have Priory Park," recalled City and Sussex centre half **Gordon Randall**. "As United got into debt and lasted only a few seasons the upheaval served no real purpose. It was a great pity, when we were getting good gates in Priory Park."

Bert 'Sticky' Glue, goalkeeper, team captain and Club Patron: "Losing our Priory Park ground was a bitter blow, the worst since the Club's formation in 1881."

City player-coach Jock Basford (successor to the first player-coach Jock Anderson) broke away from City following disagreements and set up United with insurance agent Bunny Jackson as secretary. They felt Chichester warranted better class football.

But they were refused entry to the Metropolitan League. In spite of this, they launched an offer of 10s. shares to float a limited company.

City councillors were left to decide which club should use Priory Park. To City's dismay in 1955, when rivalry was intense, they gave both equal rights, but ruled that the Park could not be closed for a gate. Town Clerk Banks had found out that it should never be closed more than 12 times a year.

It looked as if there would be an explosive situation with both clubs turning up for the same pitch until the Council arranged two pitches in Oaklands Park, the United's where tennis and golf is now played.

United struggled with poor support and no regular income. By 1957 they had left County League Division 2 and were just in West Sussex League Division 2. Basford departed for Southern League Guildford as coach, trainer and physio'.

Owing money and unable to keep the ground going, United terminated its lease in 1958. The dream was over. It had cost £1,750 to put up a pavilion and fencing and plumb in water and drainage.

Chichester City with the two main Sussex trophies - Royal Ulster Rifles Cup (left) and Sussex County League Championship (right). Roy Gilfillan, who came as £2 a week player-coach from Newport, IOW, led them to success after success for three years.

They won the County League twice, 1959-60 and 1960-61, and were nearly champions for a record third year. In 1960 they were joint holders of the RUR Cup and reached the first round proper of both the FA Cup and the FA Amateur Cup.

cup winners
chichester city
football club...

Left to right, standing - Derek Bailey, John Rumsey, Tony Cunningham, Peter Thomas, Fred Knott, Dave Aburrow, Stan Blythman (sponge man); seated - John Nurse, Nigel Hillier, Roy Gilfillan, Mick Blythman, Peter Harris.

Chichester in the 1950s

A strong 1956-57 Chichester City side outside Lewes pavilion.
Left to right, standing - Dave Luke, Alfie Woolcock, Peter Thomas, Gordon Randall, Alfie Davies, Bill Jeffery; seated - Mick Petter, Jimmy Offord, Derek Bailey, Roy Bayley, Terry Yearworth.

Probably 1950, Chichester City Supporters' Club gathered in the Cattle Market for a bus trip to Lewes to cheer on their team in the Sussex Senior Cup semi-final. Supporters' efforts helped provide Jock Anderson, Pompey's 1939 Cup Final centre forward, as first player-coach.

STRONG CRICKET TEAM

Priory Park cricketers enjoyed successful seasons on their picturesque ground and this 1954 team was typically strong. Ted Avery (centre) was a prolific scorer, usually knocking half-a-dozen centuries a season.

He was one of the finest club cricketers in the south.

Left to right, standing- Charlie Dowling, Arthur Holder, Eric Simmonds, Dick Longlands, Gordon Randall, Stan Doree; seated - Charles Whelan, John Brooks, Ted Avery, Fred Pearce, Ernie Stevens (West Sussex Football League Secretary).

The first team, played major Sussex towns, including Horsham, Lewes and Brighton, and was among the strongest. At 6ft.6ins. an impressive fast bowler, Longlands was captain in the Fifties. His father, Gus Longlands, had been skipper for most of the war. Ted Avery, solicitor Rodney Underhill and Ken Vaughan were also captains. Simmonds, Doree, Whelan and Brooks were batsmen, Holder a fast bowler, Pearce a left-arm medium pace bowler, Stevens a slow off-break bowler, Dowling an all-rounder and Randall wicket keeper. Roy Fielder (not pictured) was a good all-rounder.

Chichester Nomads, a Sunday side, amalgamated with Priory Park and, when the Hockey Club joined in, it became Priory Park Cricket and Hockey Club.

NOMADS WERE BUSINESSMEN

Members of Chichester Nomads Cricket Club, were local businessmen. In the summer they shut up shop for Thursday half-day closing and played cricket. Pictured here on a visit to Brussels (date unknown)

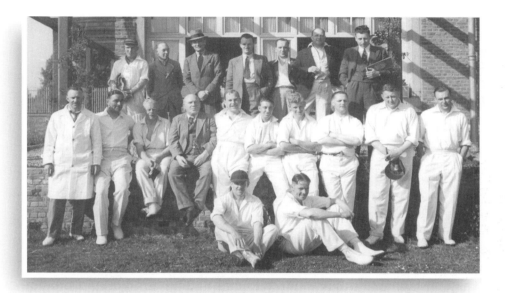

Left to right: **Back row** - ?, Frank Bushby, Tom Kimbell, John Palmer, Les Hooker, ?, Henry Gardner; **Middle row** - ?, Gus Longlands, Charles Goodger, David Kimbell, Tom Hooker, Sid Clark, John Lock, Charlie Foster, ?, ?; **Seated** - Bert Ruffell, Matt Rasell.

COUNTY CRICKET LOST

Cricket lovers were sorry when Sussex Cricket Club called off their annual Cricket Week in Priory Park.

Support fell away and the number at the matches against Oxford University and Glamorgan in June 1950 numbered only 2,600.

Crowds watching the City Band and ATC Squadron Band lead out the carnival procession from the Market on June 24 were disappointed to see fewer entries. The last Carnival Queen was 20-year-old Audrey Dale. Selected at a dance earlier in the month, she was crowned by Sussex skipper Jim Langridge during an interlude at the Gaumont.

Some of the cricket was interesting, Cox and Oakes striking Sussex centuries, but both matches petered out in draws, leaving spectators, particularly at the Glamorgan match, angry at the stonewalling tactics.

No-one could pretend it was a successful week. Match attendances were down by 2,000, perhaps due, to some extent, to the televising of the second Test Match.

BUSMAN'S CRICKET TEAM

Southdown Bus Inspector George Gilbert (left) with members of the Gilbertian Cricket Club, which he founded to give budding cricketers a game.

They are pictured here with umpire Charlie Newell for a match at Leigh Park in 1957 or 1958.

Left to right: Standing - John Ferguson, Dave Collyns, Ken Barber, Peter Street, Tony Smart, Ken Hoad (wicket keeper);
Kneeling - Michael Barratt, Roy Dynes, Peter Billings (captain), Philip Glue, Tony Beale.

Now Club President, Peter Street was a high scoring left-hand opening batsman. Tony Smart was a successful bowler and had trials for Sussex.

LADIES ON TARGET

Women archers shot to prominence as the City took up the ancient sport of archery. An advertisement calling an inaugural meeting in 1954 led to the formation of Chichester Bowmen. The ladies achieved distinction, Pat Fielder and Eve Burgess each becoming Chichester champions and Sussex champions.

Mrs. Fielder took part in events all over the country and underwent trials for England. Her late husband, Peter, leading sportsman and businessman, became Club secretary and helped raise a lot of money for targets and other necessities.

Mrs. Burgess, wife of City Water Engineer, Alfred Burgess, displayed on her quiver an imposing collection of awards gained in national and continental matches.

Club membership quickly built up in the decade from an initial dozen or so to over 100. Chairman J. Poate, who called the inaugural meeting, was pleased with progress and improving standards.

After the Club moved its range to the lower end of Oaklands Park it acquired the Rugby Club's old hut for its headquarters. In those days members could equip themselves with a bow, arrows and other items for about £30.

Mrs. Tessa Fowler's French Poodle pictured with lady members of Chichester Bowmen on their Oaklands Park range during the early Fifties:

Left to right, standing - Eve Burgess, Carol Pine, Pat Fielder, Ivy Harvey, Molly Beamix-Smith, Mildred Price, Tessa Fowler, Mrs. Poate; seated - Jan Harvey (Junior champion).

BOY BOXERS EXCELLED

Boxing was a strong feature of Chichester Boys' Club, thanks to the efforts of auctioneer Dick Keating.

Regular tournaments held in a ring set up in the Little London premises attracted many enthusiastic spectators.

By 1955, when the annual tournament (at Chichester Barracks) was attended by a capacity crowd of 600, the City had become a big boxing centre.

Among the Club's best fighters were J. Weller, Jimmy Reece, Bruce Woodcock, B. Toop, D. Anscombe, D. Ambrose and P. Cate. Some competed in Area and All-England youth championships.

MAYORESS OPENS BOWLS SEASON

Eyes firmly on the jack, Mayoress Ivy Pope bowled the first wood to open Priory Park Bowling Club's season at the end of the decade. Garage proprietor Bill Pope, in black homburg, was Mayor in 1959-60 and enjoyed the unique distinction for an ex-RAF man of presenting the Freedom of the City to RAF Tangmere.

To the right, in front, are Archie Tilling (secretary), Ernie Collett (captain) and Charles Stokes (vice captain). Mr. Stokes was Woolworths manager.

The year 1955 was one of the Club's most successful. Four members, R. Davies, H. Burbage, J. Arnell and S. Wooster, were chosen to play for Sussex.
An honours board was presented by W.J. Norris in 1952 to record the names of presidents and captains. Presidents in the Fifties were W.R. Lake, R. Davies, E. Voke, A. Pink, E. Payne, E. Collett, H. Burbage, N. Panchen and T. Chase.

THE HOMELESS CORMORANTS

The Cormorant Swimming Club was formed in 1956, but the long years of waiting for a Chichester pool went on until the conversion of the Eastgate Square Gaumont Cinema in 1968.

Members were frustrated because numbers were growing fast (180 by 1957) and they had to hire coaches from Everymans Garage to go to neighbouring pools for weekly practice.

Here, they are at Middleton Holiday Camp in 1957. Club Chairman Ronald Edgar (left) was a swimming official at the 1948 Olympic Games and past president of the Surrey Swimming and Water Polo Association and of the London Water Polo League. He served on the executive of Southern Counties Amateur Swimming Association.

Next to Mr. Edgar is Mrs. A. Derbyshire, past president of Southern Counties A.S.A., who went to many Olympics as chaperon or official. Just to the right is Police Inspector Leslie Rush, Club life saving instructor, and Frank Breakspeare, Club coach.

Also in the picture is Club treasurer Charles Brooker, Midland Bank Manager; Eva Edgar, who captained England at water polo; Denise St. Aubyn Hubbard, who as Denise Newman, was an international swimmer and Olympic diver; and Belle White, a 1912 and Twenties Olympic diver.

TENNIS 'TERRIER'

A very strong and successful Fifties Chichester tennis team:
Left to right, standing - Derek Arnell, Les Upperton, Fred Ifield;
seated - Lily Lloyd, Peggy Harris, Joyce Montgomerie.
Members of the former Whyke Tennis Club, they are pictured
after beating Petworth by six matches to three.
Peggy Harris , known as the 'Terrier' because of the way she ran for everything, played for 40 years.

A RILEY IN AN EAST STREET PARKING AREA OPPOSITE TIMOTHY WHITES AND TAYLORS, WHICH BECAME BOOTS STORE. A TRAFFIC SIGN DIRECTED A27 AND MIDHURST TRAFFIC ROUND THE CROSS.

LONG LOST BUSINESSES IN THIS AREA OF NORTH STREET- SINGER SEWING MACHINE COMPANY; HARRY LUDLOW (LEATHER SELLER); D. COMBES (SEED MERCHANT); GUY REYNOLDS (MENS' OUTFITTER); WILLIAM CLARK (DECORATORS SUPPLIES); GEERINGS (DRAPERS); AND CHARLIE HOWARD (BUTCHER).

Give yourself a
champion's chance
with . . .

Dunlop
TENNIS EQUIPMENT

TENNIS BALLS:
Dunlop Fort .. 3/3 ea.
Dunlop Warwick 2/6 ea.
(including P.T.)

DUNLOP TENNIS RACKETS:
A range of ten models which contains a model for every player and purse from 50/- to 136/6 (including P.T.)

DUNLOP ALPHA RACKETS — a lightweight Model designed specially for Juniors and Beginners. Exceptional Value: 42/-

Russell Hillsdon

The Sports store of the South

46 SOUTH STREET — CHICHESTER
Tels. 3811/2

'SUSSEX WON'T BE DRUV,'

*Some folks 'as come to Sussex
They reckons as they know
A darn sight better what to do
Than silly folks like me and you
Could possibly suppose*

*But them 'as come to Sussex
They musn't push and shove,
For Sussex will be Sussex
And Sussex won't be druv.*

VICTOR COOK
Chichester Journalist, Poet and Author.

*SHOPS CHANGED HANDS BUT TIGHT PLANNING LAWS ENSURED THE
PRESERVATION OF THESE EAST STREET FRONTAGES.*

"TIME TO SERVICE MY LIGHTS
- IT'S A LIGHT SERVICE COST"

Bring your commercial vehicles in to have their
electrical systems checked *now*, and avoid the more
costly repairs so often made necessary by winter
hazards. Headlights should be aligned and focused;
spot lamps and fog lamps correctly fitted or adjusted.
Check should be made on generator charging rate . . .
battery condition . . . and fan belt adjustment.
We can do this for you quickly and economically.

**Your Ford Dealer for Servicing all
Thames Vehicles:**

D. Rowe & Co Ltd

THE HORNET, CHICHESTER
TELEPHONE No.1 2471 (3 lines)

POWER PAK
HAND BUILT 49 CC BICYCLE MOTOR

THE ONLY MOTOR
WITH A 12 MONTHS GUARANTEE
25 GUINEAS (TERMS AVAILABLE)

A. ANDREWS
13, NORTH STREET,
CHICHESTER
'Phone 2060

RAILINGS WERE PUT UP IN PRIORY PARK SO EVERYONE COULD SEE THE QUEEN
DURING THE 1956 ROYAL VISIT.
THE QUEEN WISHED THE CITY PROSPERITY AND SUCCESS.

LOOKING ALONG NORTH STREET FROM THE SHOE SHOP OF STEAD AND SIMPSON LTD. ON THE CITY CROSS CORNER (LATE FIFTIES) - OSBORNES STORES; PAT AUSTIN'S WOOL SHOP; H. ROGERS, WATCH MAKER; P.L. HUGGINS, NEWSAGENT; SHIRLEYS, DRAPERS; C. HENDRY, MEN'S AND BOYS' OUTFITTERS; SIDNEY BASTOW, CHEMIST; AND WOOLWORTHS.

ON HORSEBACK, JEREMY GOODGER PINK CARRIED THE CITY CHARTER OF 1685 FOR THE OPENING OF THE MEMORABLE FESTIVAL OF BRITAIN (1951) IN EASTGATE SQUARE.

THANK YOU VERY MUCH

I wish to thank all the kind people who have helped in the preparation of this book by willingly giving information, advice and encouragement. My wife, Irene, who has accompanied me on interviews and research, has shown forbearance with my pre-occupation, computer tip-tapping and odd hours.

A picture is worth a thousand words, so the loan of photographs by the individuals mentioned in the pages has been invaluable. Particular thanks are due to Ken Green, local historian and the author of four books (the latest on Chichester street names), Chichester City Council, the Cathedral Dean and Chapter, Stride and Son, Terence Banks and Keith Smith, railway historian and author of 100 books on railways.

The County Record Office has been very ready to assist.

While backround information from the Chichester Observer and other publications has been helpful, it is the personal memories of survivors which have provided the details, atmosphere and colour of those times. So thanks go to all those quoted in the pages, too numerous to list, who have freely given time for a chat about times past.

The technicalities of modern book production are many and intricate. Norman Rhodes (manager) and staff at the County Council Print Unit and Jason Millington, proprietor of Melrose Computers, Bognor Regis, have always been willing to help this novice.

Thank you everybody.

Edward Brown

First published 1996

By EB Publications,
48 Grosvenor Road,
Chichester,
West Sussex. PO19 2RX

Telephone: 01243 783964

Designed by
David Moxey @ W.S.C.C. The Print Unit.

Printed by
West Sussex County Council, The Print Unit, The Tannery, Westgate, Chichester, PO19 3RH.